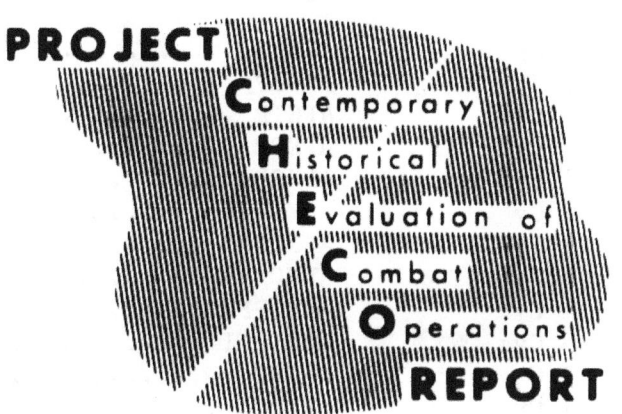

PROJECT CHECO REPORT
Contemporary Historical Evaluation of Combat Operations

OPERATION
PAUL REVERE/SAM HOUSTON
27 July 1967

HQ PACAF

Directorate, Tactical Evaluation
CHECO Division

Prepared by:
Mr. Lawrence J. Hickey
S.E. Asia Team

DISTRIBUTION PAGE

HQ USAF

AFAMA	1 Cy	AFSMS	1 Cy
AFBSA	1 Cy	AFSLP	1 Cy
AFCHO	2 Cys	AFSTP	1 Cy
AFFRA	1 Cy	AFXOP	1 Cy
AFGOA	2 Cys	AFXOPA	1 Cy
AFIGO	1 Cy	AFXOPFL	1 Cy
AFIIN	1 Cy	AFXOPFN	1 Cy
AFIAS	1 Cy	AFXOPFR	1 Cy
AFISL	1 Cy	AFXOPFH	1 Cy
AFNINDE	3 Cys	AFXOPFI	1 Cy
AFNINCC	1 Cy	AFXPD	9 Cys
AFNINA	1 Cy	AFXDOC	1 Cy
AFOMO	1 Cy	AFXDOD	1 Cy
AFPDP	1 Cy	AFXDOL	1 Cy
AFRDC	1 Cy	SAFOI	2 Cys
AFRDR	1 Cy	SAFLL	1 Cy
AFRDQ	1 Cy	SAFAA	1 Cy
AFSDC	1 Cy		

AIR UNIVERSITY

ASI-HA	2 Cys	AUL3T-66-7	1 Cy
ASI-ASAD	1 Cy	ACSC	1 Cy

MAJCOM

TAC (DPLPO)	2 Cys	AFLC (MCF)	1 Cy
9AF	1 Cy	ATC (ATXDC)	1 Cy
12AF (DAMR-C)	1 Cy	SAC (DCS/I)	1 Cy
19AF (DA-C)	1 Cy	SAC (DXIH)	1 Cy
USAFSAWC	1 Cy	SAC (DPL)	1 Cy
USAFTAWC (DA)	1 Cy	USAFE (OPL)	2 Cys
USAFTARC	1 Cy	USAFSO (NDI)	1 Cy
USAFTALC	1 Cy	USAFSO (BIOH)	1 Cy
USAFTFWC (CA)	1 Cy		
MAC (MAXDC)	1 Cy		
AFSC (SCL)	1 Cy		

OTHERS

SR AFREP (SW)	1 Cy
AFAITC	1 Cy
FTD (TDFC)	1 Cy

HQ PACAF

C	1 Cy	IG	1 Cy
DOP	1 Cy	DXIH	1 Cy
DP	1 Cy	5AF (DOP)	1 Cy
DI	1 Cy	13AF (DPL)	1 Cy
DO	1 Cy	7AF (CHECO)	9 Cys
DM	1 Cy	DTEC	3 Cys
DPL	1 Cy		

TABLE OF CONTENTS

	Page
FOREWORD	v
INTRODUCTION	vii

CHAPTER I - OPERATION PAUL REVERE I (10 May - 31 Jul 66) 1

Background	1
Initial Contacts (10 - 27 May)	2
LZ 10 Alpha (28 - 29 May)	3
Light Contact (30 May - 23 Jun)	6
Border Fire Fight (24 June)	7
Renewed Contact (3 July)	8
Results	9

CHAPTER II - OPERATION PAUL REVERE II (1 - 25 Aug 66) 11

Background	11
Initial Contact and Buildup (1 - 2 Aug)	12
Challenge (2 Aug)	13
Search and Maneuver (3 - 7 Aug)	15
Shift to Southwest; Search of River Valleys (8 - 12 Aug)	17
Search of Chu Pong and Border (13 - 21 Aug)	20
Results of PAUL REVERE II	24
Summary of Air Support	24

CHAPTER III - OPERATION PAUL REVERE III (26 Aug - 17 Oct 66) 28

3/25th Div Operations (27 Aug - 17 Oct)	28
Operation 50 (11 - 17 Oct)	29
Results of Operation 50	33
Final Results Operation PAUL REVERE III	34

CHAPTER IV - OPERATION PAUL REVERE IV (18 Oct - 31 Dec 66) 35

New Buildup	35
Deployment and Initial Contact (18 - 29 Oct)	35
The Search Steps Up (30 Oct - 8 Nov)	39
Deployment Across Nam Sathay (9 - 10 Nov)	40
Task Force PRONG in Trouble (11 Nov)	44
Reinforcement (11 - 12 Nov)	48
All Out Attack (12 - 13 Nov)	53
The Search Continues (13 - 20 Nov)	62
Arc Light Routes the Enemy (20 - 24 Nov)	63
Contact Continues (20 - 21 Nov)	64
Enemy Attack in South (21 Nov)	65
Final Phases (22 Nov - 31 Dec)	68
PAUL REVERE IV Results	70

	Page
CHAPTER V - OPERATION SAM HOUSTON (1 Jan - 5 Apr 67)	72
Background	72
The Enemy Returns (14 - 18 Feb)	73
Reinforcement and Search (17 Feb - 5 Apr)	79
Results and Analysis of Operation SAM HOUSTON	83
Conclusion	89

FOOTNOTES

    Chapter I 91
    Chapter II 93
    Chapter III 96
    Chapter IV 97
    Chapter V 102

APPENDIXES

    I -- USAF SUPPORT OF PAUL REVERE II 105
    II -- USAF SUPPORT OF PAUL REVERE IV 106
    III -- USAF SUPPORT OF SAM HOUSTON 107

GLOSSARY 109

FIGURES   Follows Page

1. Landing Zone 4
2. Operation PAUL REVERE I 6
3. Operation PAUL REVERE II 16
4. Operation PAUL REVERE IV 54
5. B-52 Bomber Strikes, Operation PAUL REVERE IV 68
6. Area of Operation, Operation SAM HOUSTON 72
7. A-1 Covers Landing Zone 74
8. Landing Zone Area 76
9. B-52 Strike Areas, Operation SAM HOUSTON 86

FOREWORD

This study covers a year of tough fighting in the highly strategic central highlands area of Vietnam, an area which the communists have always considered essential to their effort to take over South Vietnam. Prior to the arrival of U.S. forces in 1965, there was little activity in western Pleiku Province, but starting with the move of the 1st Air Cavalry Division to the defense of the besieged fort of Plei Me in October 1965, fighting has been continuous. The western Pleiku area, however, on the western end of strategic Highway 19, which cuts across the country to the coastal port of Qui Nhon, is the logical entry point for any planned enemy drive to cut South Vietnam in half. In this objective, the enemy has not succeeded.

What emerges clearly from this account of fighting by the 1st Air Cav, 25th, and 4th Infantry Divisions in the central highlands is the absolute essentiality of air support to survival of the friendly forces. Perhaps never in history has a large ground force in war been so dependent upon air support, close air support, and tactical airlift, as well as other air support functions such as interdiction, landing zone preparation, reconnaissance, night flare drops, defoliation, psy-war and search-and-rescue.

This study shows in detail the means by which air was employed in the highlands fighting and how it directly affected and influenced the ground action. The U.S. units are generally flown to the battle areas and are cut off by land from their normal support bases. They cannot continue to function effectively without the air umbrella provided by the vast armada of U.S. aircraft located in Vietnam. Air support, as can be seen from this study, is infinitely more than a new dimension of artillery.

It is the difference between success or failure and no one will attest to this more strongly than the U.S. Army ground commanders on the receiving end, many of whom are quoted in the study.

This study is also a lucid testimonial to the exceptional professionalism and bravery exhibited by the Air Force men who flew the O-1 FAC planes, the A-1E, F-100, B-57, and F-4C strike aircraft, the C-123 and C-130 airlift planes, the AC-47 flareships, and the rescue helicopters. They were carving out a new role for airpower in an environment which favored the enemy's classical tactics of guerrilla warfare. And they were proving that in Vietnam, as in the skies over Germany and Korea, air is the essential, and decisive, element of warfare.

INTRODUCTION

The southern terminus of one of the branches of the Ho Chi Minh Trail, western Pleiku and Kontum Provinces, was one of the first areas of South Vietnam to see a significant buildup of North Vietnamese Regular Army units. Control of this area has always been imperative to the free infiltration of men and supplies from the North into the Central Highlands of the South, and this relatively uninhabited area with its small aboriginal population, is well suited to the introduction of large numbers of North Vietnamese Army (NVA) troops.

This area is mainly peopled by a few thousand primitive Montagnard tribesmen who live a seminomadic life of subsistence by farming and hunting. Vegetation is extremely heavy throughout the area with a predominance of double and triple canopied rain forest. The terrain is rugged and ranges from densely forested mountains and plateaus to large river valleys fed by innumerable rushing torrents which drain the elevated areas. Concealment is excellent and the enemy has crisscrossed the entire region with numerous highspeed trails which greatly facilitate enemy movement through the area.

Initially, a small string of Special Forces (SF) Camps, each defended by a handful of Special Forces Advisors and a couple of hundred Montagnard Civilian Irregular Defense Group (CIDG) soldiers, was scattered along the border to monitor and control enemy movement. Often these camps constitute the only government influence in the entire area. In western Pleiku and Kontum Provinces, there are four such camps: Plei Me, Plei Djereng,

Plei Mrong and Duc Co. While these camps could not control the influx of enemy troops and supplies across the border, they were a source of constant annoyance to the enemy and did prevent the entirely unimpeded control of the area by the communists.

When the communists were ready to open an all out offensive to take control of South Vietnam during the summer of 1965, their strategy called for a drive across the Central Highlands along Highway 19, which would cut South Vietnam in two and isolate the northern half of the country. To accomplish this objective, the 325th NVA Division was poised on the Vietnamese-Cambodian border, ready to launch the attack.

The Duc Co Special Forces Camp was apparently the first objective of this offensive, which was thrown off schedule when a government spoiling operation in early August, forced the enemy's hand and cost him heavy casualties. 1/ The offensive was finally launched in mid-October, with the first division-sized operation of the war against the Plei Me Special Forces Camp. 2/ The battle raged for ten days before the vanquished enemy finally withdrew, having suffered as many as 2,000 casualties.

For the next several weeks, the fleeing enemy was pursued by the 1st Air Cavalry Division (ACD) in Operations LONG REACH and SILVER BAYONET. 3/ Together, these two operations, reaching a climax in the bloody encounters along the Ia Drang River, cost the enemy an additional two- to three-thousand casualties and the U.S. forces more than five hundred. In November 1965, the 1st ACD terminated the operation rather than force a showdown in such difficult terrain on the enemy's own terms. The enemy had failed to accomplish his objectives and had taken severe losses but he still controlled the border area. Furthermore, his bases remained intact.

By May 1966, U.S. manpower in Vietnam had increased enough to have the 3d Brigade of the 25th Division committed to prolonged operations in the area. Operation PAUL REVERE was initiated and continued through several phases until the end of the year. In October, the 2d Brigade, 4th Division took control of the area from their permanent base camp near Plei Djereng and the 25th Division withdrew most of its forces from the area.

PAUL REVERE and its successors, Operations SAM HOUSTON and FRANCIS MARION, through the middle of May 1967, had accounted for at least 7,000 enemy casualties and repeatedly disrupted enemy plans and activities in the area. The entire area of operations (AO) had been thoroughly searched at least once and most of the old permanent-type enemy base camps had been uncovered and destroyed.

When ejected from his base areas, however, the enemy adopted a now familiar pattern of activity. From secure base camps and supply depots, behind the immunity of the Cambodian border, the enemy periodically moved large numbers of troops—one to two divisions—across the border to launch an offensive, each time with the initial objective of a Special Forces Camp. The buildup was always compromised by Special Forces patrols and U.S. border surveillance programs. This led to a major confrontation in a series of bloody battles. The overwhelming mobility and fire support of Allied Forces were always the deciding factors, and badly beaten, the enemy retreated across the border to rest, resupply, and reinforce before returning to Vietnam and initiating the cycle again. Since May 1966, this had happened at least five times.

This tactic cost the enemy repeated failures and heavy losses, but as long as the integrity of his Cambodian bases was maintained and his will to prolong the struggle endured, there could be no forseeable conclusion to the contest for control of this important area.

> "You don't fight this fellow rifle to rifle. You locate him and back away. Blow the hell out of him and then police up." 1/
> --Brigadier General Glenn D. Walker
> ADC, 4th Infantry Division

CHAPTER I

OPERATION PAUL REVERE I
(10 May-31 July 1966)

Background

PAUL REVERE I was initiated on 10 May 1966, as a search-and-destroy/border surveillance operation in the Chu Pong Mountain area of Pleiku Province. Simultaneously, six CIDG Companies and the 23d Army Republic of Vietnam (ARVN) Battalion launched a coordinated sweep known as Than Phong 14, within the same tactical area of responsibility (TAOR). 2/

The operation was started by the 3d Brigade, 25th Division (3/25th Div), which committed three infantry battalions (1/35,2/35,1/14) with supporting tanks and artillery. 3/ On 29 May, this force was additionally reinforced by the 2d Brigade, 1st Air Cavalry Division (ACD) with two battalions (2/5,2/12). However, the 2d Bde, 1st ACD was withdrawn on 10 June, to conduct Operation HOOKER I in the AO between Operations PAUL REVERE and HAWTHORNE. 4/ In addition, during the period 23 May through 18 June, Project DELTA, a Special Forces intensive reconnaissance operation, directly supported PAUL REVERE I. 5/

Initial Contacts (10 - 27 May)

The 3d Brigade, 25th Division made no significant contact through the first two weeks of operations. Air support was employed, however, whenever needed and a flight of 366th Tactical Fighter Wing (TFW) F-4Cs, striking an enemy concentration some six miles west of Duc Co Special Forces Camp on 13 May, was later credited by a USSF body-count (evaluated C-3) with 100 enemy killed by air (KBA). 6/

Two CIDG Companies made heavy contact with an estimated two NVA Battalions five miles southwest of Plei Djereng SF Camp on 24 May. The CIDGs, who were on their way back to camp after a patrol, requested Capt. Joseph A. Machowski, a Pleiku Sector Forward Air Controller (FAC), to divert from his visual reconnaissance (VR) mission and fly air cover for them. For the next 90 minutes, Captain Machowski flew ahead of the ground force, scouting for a possible ambush. Suddenly, he spotted an estimated two battalions of NVA in ambush positions just ahead of the friendly ground force. 7/

The FAC immediately swung into action. He notified the ground force of the ambush, called for air strikes, and then proceeded to disrupt the ambush by firing smoke rockets and dropping smoke grenades into the enemy positions. The fighters soon arrived and began expending on the enemy force, which was by now attempting to annihilate the friendly patrol. 8/

Captain Machowski's Silver Star citation recorded the action. 9/

> "With complete disregard for his own personal safety he
> directed numerous combat sorties against this opposing

> force, constantly subjecting himself to hostile machine
> gun and automatic weapons fire. After the first flight
> of fighters had expended their ordnance and pending a
> subsequent flight, Captain Machowski made continual low
> passes over the hostile positions to harrass (sic) the
> enemy to keep them from overrunning the friendly posi-
> tions. Upon arrival of more fighter aircraft he sys-
> tematically destroyed enemy positions in order that the
> ground troops could have sufficient time to regroup their
> units and attain a more viable defensive position pending
> the arrival of reinforcements for a successful counter-
> attack... He was so successful that air strikes were
> laid within 100 meters of friendly positions and were
> effective in discouraging enemy units from reforming
> for counter moves. ...Discovery of this multi-battalion
> force and the ensuing battle that lasted for a day and a
> half with 18 combat sorties being flown during the time,
> prevented or delayed a large scale attack on a Special
> Forces camp which the ground commanders acknowledged as
> a prelude to major enemy offensive actions in the Central
> Highlands during the current monsoon season."

Captain Machowski continued his mission until enemy ground fire blasted his O-1F out of the sky. The FAC succeeded in gliding his damaged craft to a crash-landing in a banana grove. Signal mirror flashes were initially observed near the wreckage from rescue aircraft, but they suddenly ceased and the helicopters were driven off by heavy ground fire. More than 90 minutes elapsed before rescuers finally reached the downed FAC, who died from three bullet wounds through the neck. [10]/

Six A-1E and two F-4C sorties on 24 May, in support of this action, netted a total of 27 NVA killed by air (KBA) according to a U.S. Special Forces body-count. [11]/

LZ 10 Alpha (28 - 29 May)

Heavy contact was again made on 28 May, when 2/35th was ambushed by an element of the 33d NVA Regiment as it air-assaulted into landing zone (LZ) 10 Alpha, about five miles north of Duc Co. The incoming assault helicopters were raked with fire from at least five 12.7-mm antiaircraft machine guns, four of which were mounted in the trees a short distance northeast of the LZ. Before these guns could be knocked out by air strikes, four helicopters were shot down. 12/

Capt. Bruce Hoon was the second Forward Air Controller to be dispatched to the scene that day. At about the same time, a flight of F-4Cs, Boxer 01, arrived and the FACs began to expend their 500-pound bombs against the suspected locations of the enemy gun positions. 13/ Captain Hoon described the action this way: 14/

> "I had 20mm cannons left and I told them (the fighters) to just hold off on the 20mm while I went down to take a look for a BDA...I flew over the LZ and then turned left to the north alongside the mountain where I thought they might be.
>
> "Well, I passed this area and I couldn't see anything down there but craters and stripped trees...but as I passed the area a little bit northeast of the LZ, the aircraft kind of shook momentarily and oops, there they were again! And about four of them opened up on me. I was down about 300 or 400 feet--good duck shooting altitude--and I broke away, made a wide circle to the left, diving for the tree tops.
>
> "I was all out of smoke rockets...so I told the fighters to make a wide pattern and tack in on my tail, that I would be coming in from the west towards the east and I was down on the tree tops. I said, 'In front of me about a mile, you'll see a clearing there just to the northeast of where the friendlies are.' Being on the side of the hill, the trees made a kind of wall and I could see when I passed over this..., where the smoke was coming up when they fired at me. And I told them...: 'I don't have a mark so I'm going to have to talk you into it. Line up

LANDING ZONE
WESTERN KONTUM PROVINCE
FIGURE 1

on me, and...I'll describe it to you when you go in there and when you've got it, then I'll break to the right, over the friendlies and you just hose away.'

"He told me he did have it, so I broke to the right and he just let loose with the 20mm gattling guns that he had on board. This netted us four 12.7mm guns....

"The fifth 12.7 was located about a click and a half north of the first ones... I got a second set of fighters and the load was just perfect for it. They had a load of 220 pound frag cluster bombs and we expended both aircraft...in two passes. Each would drop two clusters at a time. One bracketed on the short side of it...; the burst radius was just all intermeshed...right where I thought the gun was. Apparently it was so because we got no more fire out of the position."

Throughout the day, the FACs continued the air strikes under a blanket clearance from the Brigade Commander to hit anything with air within a 1,500-meter radius of the LZ. Pilots were credited with two confirmed KBA by FAC body-count for these missions. [15/]

That night a C-123 flareship dropped numerous flares throughout the area to keep the battlefield lit, as action continued all night and through the next day. It was not until late on the night of 29 May, that the enemy finally broke all contact and withdrew. [16/]

During the next three days, 218 North Vietnamese bodies were found in the vicinity of the engagement and, according to Captain Hoon, subsequent discoveries of enemy grave sites over the next month raised the final enemy toll for the battle to nearly 470 KIA/KBA. [17/] Two NVA prisoners were taken during the 40-hour battle and large quantities of arms and equipment were also captured. American losses were 13 KIA and 39 WIA.[18]

Light Contact (30 May-23 Jun)

Intelligence had by this time determined that elements of three NVA Regiments were operating in the AO: the 32d, 33d, and 66th; but action tapered off to sporadic light contact as the search for the enemy continued.[19] The 2d Brigade, 1st ACD became OPCON to the 3/25th Div on 2 June, and began searching the area northwest of Duc Co as far as the Se San River. This two-battalion force with a cooperating CIDG Company made no significant contact and was withdrawn to a new operational AO on 11 June.[20]

Project DELTA teams conducted extensive reconnaissance during this period in an effort to pinpoint the major enemy forces. Team One was infiltrated on 10 June, and two days later located an abandoned enemy regimental base camp. Continuing east from this location, the team observed two halted enemy battalions which had been moving along trails in a southwesterly direction. Two air strikes were called in on the enemy's position and two secondary explosions occurred, but the team was unable to confirm the number of enemy casualties.[21] The next day, the team located another enemy force of from two- to three-hundred men, resting. As the small team watched the enemy and waited for the requested air strike to arrive, an eight-man enemy security patrol passed within 20 meters of their hiding place. One flight of tactical fighters was expended on the target, again with unknown results.[22]

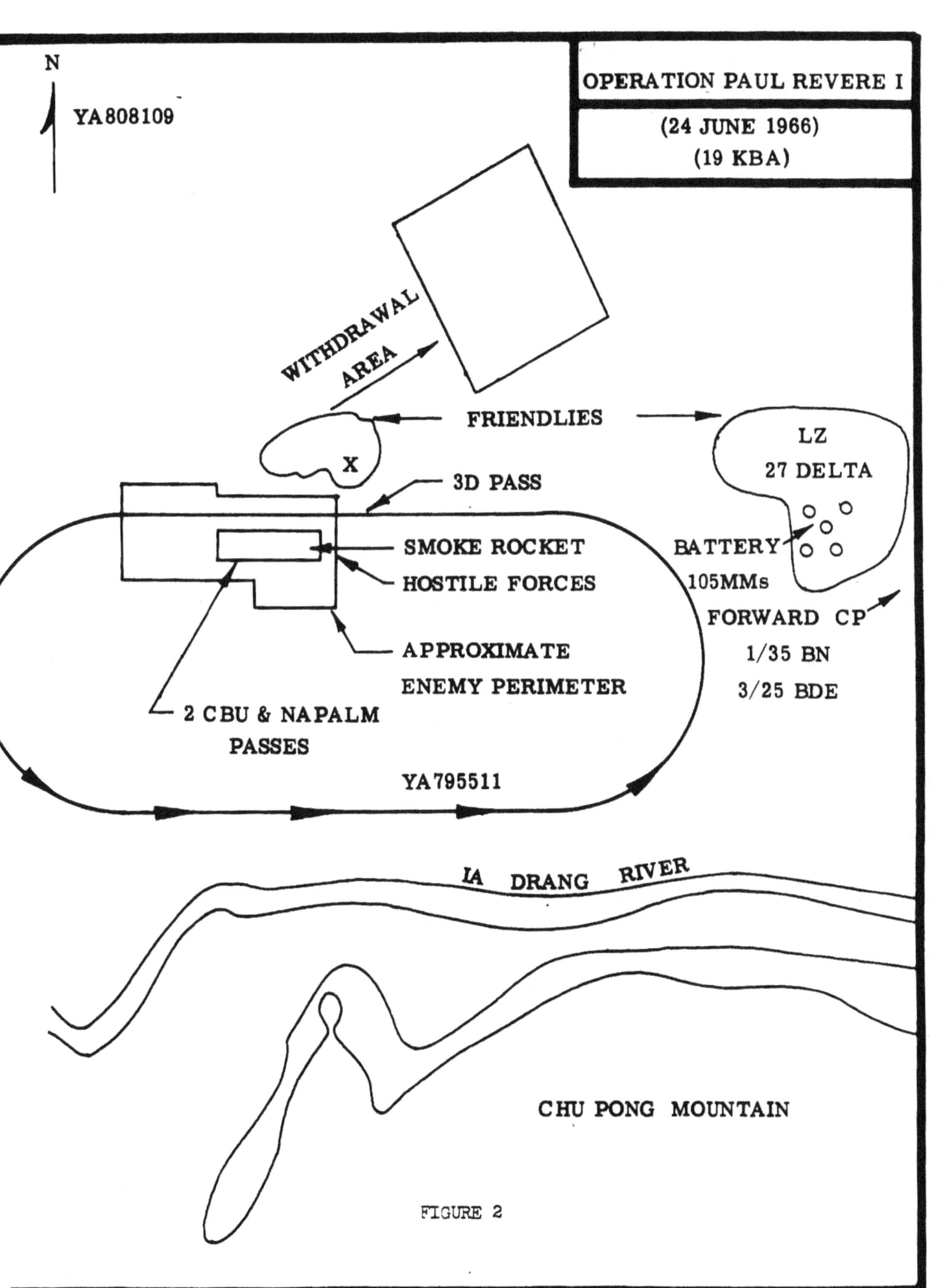

FIGURE 2

Border Fire Fight (24 June)

Shortly after 0800 hours on 24 June, a Recon Platoon from Alpha Company, 2/35, was scouting just north of the Ia Drang River, and less than a thousand yards from the Cambodian border, when they were attacked and severely mauled by a large enemy force.[23] Captain Hoon was the first FAC to reach the embattled platoon, whose situation he described as follows:[24]

> "They had the enemy located to the west and to the south of them wrapped around this tree line. Now they started receiving this small arms fire from across the cleared area and...they had our guys pretty well tied down...One Seven Alpha (the radio call-sign of the platoon leader) popped a yellow smoke for me; so it located him in the trees positively and I asked him to make sure that he gave me an idea of how far his people were spread out. He said they were in the thin trees; they were spread out roughly in a fifty to a hundred meter radius of where the smoke was. This put the enemy about a hundred and fifty meters away from them at this time.
>
> "After I put the smoke rocket in for the A-1s and they started making the passes--the first being napalm and the second aircraft coming in with CBU --the Charlies started coming out into the open... trying to close with our troops as rapidly as possible so we wouldn't deliver any more ordnance on top of them.
>
> "I told One Seven Alpha...that I could see them coming out of the trees and they were closing with them, trying to rush them...I passed the word on to the fighter aircraft and they set up their miniguns underneath the wing...
>
> "I told them...'I got about fifteen of them in the open' and lead says 'I see them down there...right along underneath the edge of the smoke.' They took about two passes, one apiece..., and we stopped all fifteen of them right there. Then they finished with the rest of the ordnance they had, spreading it around in those heavy trees."

Contact continued until around 1700 hours, when the enemy finally withdrew after being pounded by four more air strikes. When the area of contact was swept the next day, 60 enemy bodies were still on the battlefield and from blood stains and bloody trails, it appeared that this was only a small portion of the enemy casualties. Nineteen of the enemy bodies were credited by the Army as KBA, including the 15 mowed down by the 1st Air Commando Squadron's A-1Es.[25] Initial reports listed friendly casualties for the day as three KIA, 26 WIA, and 11 MIA.[26]

Renewed Contact (3 July)

The enemy avoided contact until 3 July, when an element of 1/35th made two heavy contacts with an NVA Force about six miles south of Duc Co. Capt. Hubert E. Thornber, Jr. relieved the first FAC, who was running low on fuel, and therefore unable to finish the flight of F-4Cs he was controlling. Flying over the enemy positions, Captain Thornber came under heavy automatic weapons fire from numerous enemy gun positions.[27]

After calling for two more flights of fighters, the FAC then rolled in and marked the target through a hail of small arms fire. The F-4Cs succeeded in silencing three automatic weapons positions with their remaining ordnance before departing. A few minutes later, the two flights of A-1Es arrived and the FAC again went down to take a look. The enemy was attempting to outflank the friendly positions, so Captain Thornber brought the air strikes to within 50 meters, while he flew over the friendly positions as a mark for the fighters to prevent their expending too close.

The enemy maneuver was repulsed by the air strikes and ground forces. The battered enemy force withdrew under a devastating bombardment which inflicted heavy casualties. Captain Thornber led the strikes against the retreating enemy, by making simulated strafing attacks, with the fighters following him in trail.[28]

The day's action had been costly for the American unit, which initially reported one KIA, 28 WIA, and 16 MIA. The enemy also suffered heavy losses under the heavy pounding caused by repeated air attacks. Brig. Gen. Glenn D. Walker, the 3/25th Division's Commanding General, extended his personal thanks for the "excellent air work" in a message to the FAC on the following day. For his part in the action, Captain Thornber was awarded the Distinguished Flying Cross.[29]

Results

Operation PAUL REVERE I terminated at midnight on 31 July, with no further significant contact. PAUL REVERE II began immediately.[30]

Enemy losses were substantial, with 546 confirmed KIA, 68 captured, 39 suspects detained, and equipment losses of 224 individual, and 17 crew-served weapons. Friendly personnel losses were 66 KIA, 320 WIA, two MIA; material losses included 23 individual, and three crew-served weapons.[31]

The hundreds of tactical air sorties had provided the critical difference between victory and possible defeat in each of the three major battles of the operation, and a total of 65 enemy were confirmed KBA in support of American forces during the operation.[32] Twenty-four supporting Arc Light sorties were expended during July, and although at least one strike badly damaged a large enemy base camp, no significant results were recorded due to the absence of a ground follow-up. 33/

CHAPTER II

OPERATION PAUL REVERE II
(1 - 25 August 1966)

Background

By late July 1966, intelligence gained through PAUL REVERE I indicated that two NVA Divisions, the 625th and the 630th, were preparing to launch a major offensive to coincide with the arrival of the southwest monsoon season, a time when air support would be severely limited by marginal flying conditions throughout much of the Central Highlands. [1]

Subsequent operations determined that a multiregimental attack was scheduled against the Duc Co SF Camp for mid-August, when elaborate ambushes were to be sprung against reinforcements rushing to defend the camp. This was essentially the same strategy employed during the siege of Plei Me SF Camp in October 1965, with the only major difference being the use of two divisions in the Duc Co offensive instead of one. It was also believed that the attack on Duc Co was to have been part of an overall enemy offensive aimed at splitting the highlands and capturing Kontum or Pleiku City. [2]

Extremely poor weather conditions along the border during the last week of July, had limited air support to Combat Sky Spot missions. This condition was to prevail through 1 August, with a slight improvement thereafter. During this time, increasing contacts and sightings of the enemy pointed to a major attempt to infiltrate the Ia Drang Valley area, a situation which sparked the further commitment of Allied Forces into the AO to counter the threat. 3/

At this time, the 3d Bde, 1st ACD, was conducting Operation HAYES in Kontum Province with 1/7th Cav at Dak To and 2/7th Cav at Pleiku. On 30 July, the Commanding General of I Field Forces ordered that 2.7th Cav be attached to the 3d Bde, 25th Division and deployed into the PAUL REVERE AO. By 31 July, 2/7th Cav was beginning local search-and-destroy operations about 15 miles southeast of Plei Djereng and turning up signs of recent enemy activity in the area. 4/

Initial Contact and Buildup (1 - 2 Aug)

At 0515 hours on 1 August, the 32d NVA Regt initiated the first major contact of PAUL REVERE II by launching a battalion-sized attack against the positions of "A" and B/2/7th Cav at LZ 21D. Ninety rounds of mortar fire slammed into the camp, while ground forces repeatedly assaulted the perimeter. When his third major attack was repulsed two hours later, the enemy finally began withdrawing to the northwest, taking most of his casualties with him. 5/

Air Force Combat Sky Spot missions provided ten sorties during the morning against enemy withdrawal routes. The initial perimeter defense had been supported by flares and minigun fire from an AC-47. 6/ The enemy left 28 bodies on the field, but had hit the two U.S. Companies hard, inflicting five KIA and 68 WIA. 7/

That afternoon the 3d Bde, 1st ACD and 3d Bn, 1st Armored Cavalry Regt (Korean) were placed under the OPCON of the 3/25th Div. These units began deployment into the AO the same day. 8/

12

The NVA struck again at 15 minutes after midnight on 2 August, with a mortar attack against the positions of 2/7th Cav. TAC air and artillery teamed up to silence the enemy tubes.[9]

Challenge (2 Aug)

At midmorning, "A" Company (-) and the Recon Platoon of the 2/35th had just killed their second NVA, and were hot on the trail of the sole survivor of a group of NVA who had been observed earlier in the morning. The chase came to an abrupt halt at noon when the small group of Americans suddenly found itself at the edge of an occupied enemy regimental base camp. The enemy reacted quickly and the American force was soon surrounded. Almost immediately, the Commander and First Sergeant of "A" Company died under a hail of bullets, while the remaining force desperately attempted to establish a defensive perimeter.[10]

In response to an urgent plea for help, Captain Hoon was dispatched to the scene. By the time he arrived overhead in his O-1, the American force was already tragically decimated. As Captain Hoon recalled, "They called me and said they had six dead and 25 wounded already...so we called in air."[11] Air strikes were to be delayed for more than two hours, however, while a "Dustoff" medevac chopper made several fruitless attempts to evacuate the more critically wounded and dead.[12]

Artillery and mortar fire laid down a continuous barrage in support of the trapped unit, but sporadic ground fire and lack of a suitable LZ prevented evacuation of wounded. Finally the helicopter pulled off and

Captain Hoon got the artillery shut down long enough to put in a flight of A-1E Skyraiders. After this, he attempted to direct in two flights of armed helicopters and aerial rocket artillery ships, but a third flight of helicopters had appeared on the scene in the meantime and taken matters into its own hands. 13/

> "The 1st Cavalry Division had sent a brigade over for this particular operation and I had no radio contact with them at all, and they were just going to get in on the action.
>
> "So they saw the smoke and fire and everything, and just started firing in the area...without any clearance or anything like this. In fact, one of them got in the way of a strafe pass of one of the A-1Es one time, and I had to break the A-1E off to keep from shooting the chopper down."

Since Captain Hoon was running short of fuel, he turned over the second flight of A-1Es, which soon arrived on the scene, to Capt. Robert Eaglet, a 1st ACD FAC, who had flown over to give assistance. 14/

In the meantime, the 1st Air Cav was having problems of its own. Just before 1400 hours, A/2/7th Cav had air-assaulted its 3d Platoon into LZ Pink. The 26 men were immediately engaged and soon surrounded by an estimated reinforced NVA Company. Shortly thereafter, radio contact with the unit was lost. Throughout the afternoon, futile attempts were made to reinforce the platoon, and it wasn't until more than four hours had elapsed that B/1/12th Cav, which air-assaulted into a position 850 meters from the LZ, could reach the devastated platoon. Cavalry casualties for the action were 18 KIA and 8 WIA, including almost the entire platoon. The enemy failed to remove 16 bodies. [15]

Back at the battle site of the 3/25th Div, things had quieted down somewhat. The small force had finally been reinforced by C/2/35th and moved into a small LZ for the night. Just after dark, the FAC, Capt. Paul Hammer, put in another flight of A-1s under an extremely low-weather ceiling. [16]

Things remained fairly quiet until 2040 hours when the friendly positions began to receive mortar fire. An AC-47 was diverted and began expending flares overhead, but the attack gradually built up in intensity and soon the friendly perimeter was threatened. [17]

Captain Hoon reached the area at about midnight. The AC-47 had already expended his guns in a box around the American perimeter and was reloading for a third run. Just before firing the third salvo, "Spooky" picked up ground fire which he marked with a 45-minute ground flare. At this time, Capt. Kenneth B. Beaird and Capt. Peter M. Hegseth, of the 1st Air Commando Squadron, reached the target. [18]

Captain Hoon described the conditions that existed that night in a letter to the Commander of the 1st ACS, citing the two A-1 pilots for the action that followed: [19]

> "The weather was unsuitable for tactical fighter operations due to a heavy overcast, layered clouds below, and a fast moving fog bank about to engulf the target. It was further complicated by the darkness of the night and the confusing light of illumination flares being dropped approximately four miles north over another unit."

The mission became more complicated as Captain Beaird's landing gear had malfunctioned and remained locked in the down position. His airspeed indicator was also unreliable. Nevertheless, Captain Hoon began setting up the strike. [20]

On the ground, the situation was so critical that the commander had briefed the FAC over the radio in a whisper to avoid compromising the position of the Command Post. He then marked his position by using a small pen flashlight. The enemy troops could be heard shouting and screaming a couple of hundred yards north of the ground troops, apparently preparing to launch an all out assault. [21]

Captain Hoon described the air strike this way: [22]

> "I put my smoke mark in two to three hundred meters northwest of the ground flare which the AC-47 had dropped. The wind carried my smoke straight to the flare just like an arrow. At that moment the ground lit up like a Chinese New Year with small arms and automatic weapons fire.
>
> "Captain Beaird initiated the attack with napalm on three seperate (sic) passes, totally blanketing the area of the ground fire. Captain Hegseth alternated passes in the firing areas with CBU. It was not until all airdroppable ordnance had been delivered that Capt. Beaird indicated that he was having mechanical difficulties with his aircraft...It was apparent from his conversation that he had flown the entire mission with these difficulties. Capt. Beaird was unable to expend his 20mm guns because he was unable to depress the guns that far, but instead, he elected to make dry runs on the target, subjecting himself to the dwindling but still intense fire. Capt. Hegseth observed each pass and was able to pinpoint a new area for each run. This continued until there was no longer any ground fire. This was confirmed by the ground commander who said that all hostile fire had ceased.
>
> "It was heartwarming to hear the ground commander, who had

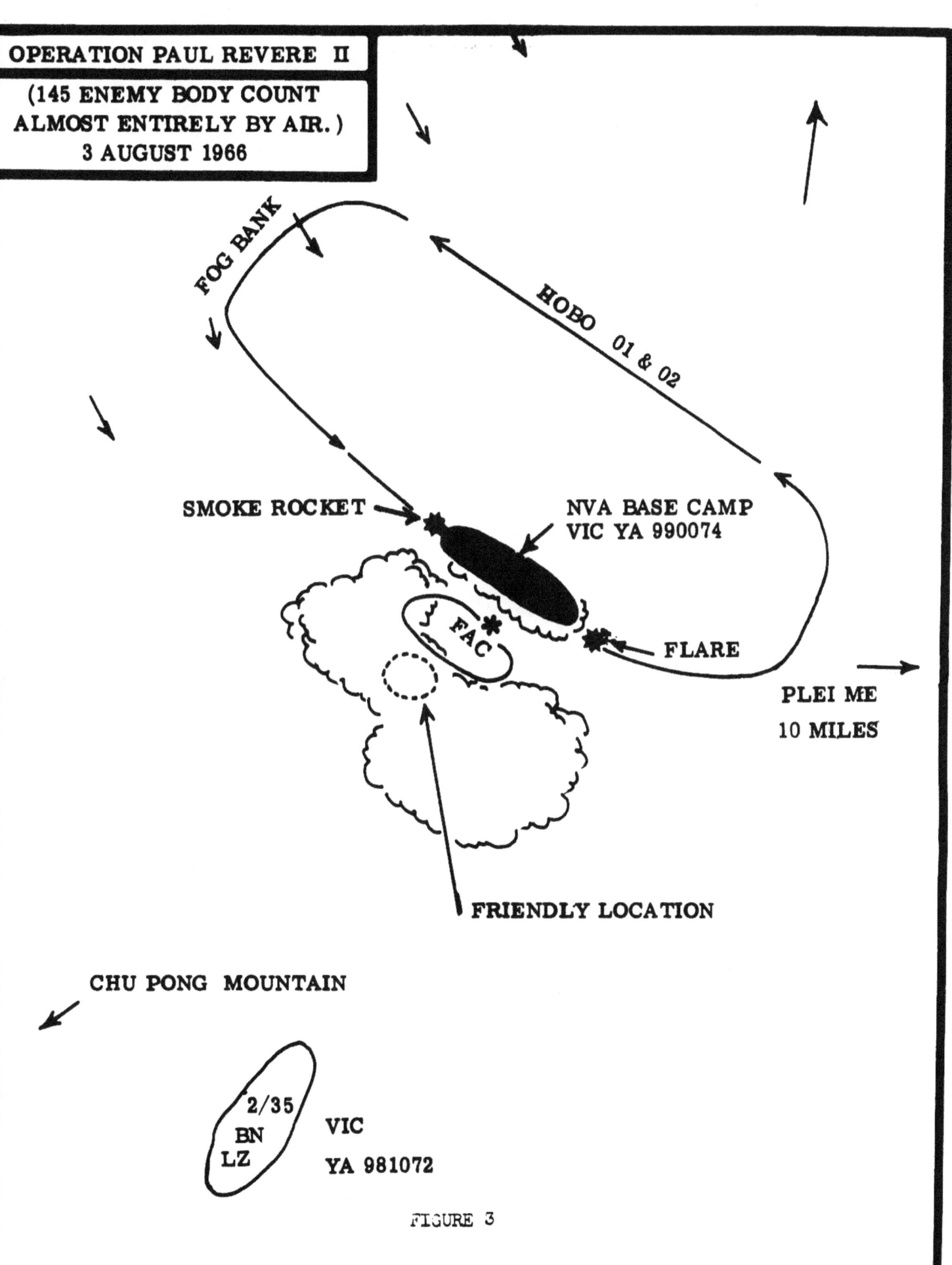

FIGURE 3

>suffered heavy casualties in the succeeding twelve hour period, say that he could rest easy for the rest of the night even though a heavy fog bank had by this time completely engulfed his position and would preclude further air activities that evening."

Captain Hoon estimated 25 KBA for the A-1E strike, but a ground search of the target the next day disclosed 145 enemy bodies. [23/] Capt. Edwin R. Maxim, another FAC for the 3/25th Div, was at the battalion headquarters during the several-hour engagement. [24/] He stated that "from our personal conversation with the Army during the following days--the Company Commander, the Battalion Commander, and Staff--the air certainly prevented an overrun and probably annihilation of the entire unit." [25/]

Search and Maneuver (3 - 7 Aug)

At 1830 hours on 2 August, OPCON of PAUL REVERE II was placed with the 1st ACD. Contact was light and scattered through 7 August, with no engagements with major enemy elements during this time. The only significant encounter was on 4 August, when C/2/5th (-) fought a late afternoon battle with an estimated reinforced enemy platoon. TAC air and Aerial Rocket Artillery (ARA) hit the area until sundown, when artillery fire was initiated under the light of a Vietnamese Air Force (VNAF) flareship. Enemy casualties from these fires were unknown. [26/]

Shift to Southwest; Search of River Valleys (8 - 12 Aug)

The 2d Brigade of the 1st ACD was added to the search forces of PAUL REVERE II beginning on 8 August. While other sources continued search operations with little contact, A/1/7th, now attached to the 2d Bde, made a small contact along the south bank of the Ia Drang River. This engagement eventually led to a major battle with what was thought to be the 4th Bn, 32d NVA Regiment. 27/

By early afternoon, heavy contact had developed. The 1st Air Cav after action report stated, "The enemy attacked in waves in their attempt to overrun the company. Artillery, ARA and TAC Air were used to great effect by the company in breaking the enemy attacks." 28/ As a result of one air strike, two A-1Hs were credited with six KBA by FAC estimate. 29/

The enemy finally broke off contact when helicopters, bringing up two reinforcing companies, whirled in overhead. The enemy was then aggressively pursued by all three companies. Total enemy losses for the encounter were 90 KIA by body-count, three NVA captured, and an estimated 196 NVA wounded. During the night, a kill zone was established over a probable enemy exfiltration route and concentrated fires of artillery and Combat Proof air strikes massively struck the area, all with unknown results. 30/

On the following day, the location of an enemy company-sized unit was pinpointed from information provided by an ambush platoon of 1/9th Cav and a POW report. According to the after action report: 31/

> "Three Sky Spots (Combat Proofs) were requested, one directly on the reported enemy and two on the most probable avenues of escape to the south and southeast. Artillery was called in sealing off the west and north. Artillery fired until the Sky Spots were dropped, then resumed firing with complete area coverage following the Sky Spots. Recon at first light disclosed no bodies, but blood, bandages, and equipment were found over the entire area. This entire support action, complete with

Sky Spots, took place in one hour and forty-two minutes."

At 2330 hours that night, a reinforced battalion of the 88th NVA Regiment launched a five-hour attack against night defense positions of the 9th Company, 3/1st Korean Regiment, and five tanks from the 1st Platoon, B/1/69th Armor (U.S.). 32/

> "Evidence was found that indicates the enemy had extensive prior planning. The attack took place either as an effort to relieve pressure from NVA units withdrawing into Cambodia or as a phase of a coordinated offensive which was spoiled by friendly forces in the Ia Drang-Chu Pong area. Due to their inherent control difficulties, cancellation could not be affected (sic)." 33/

Major Robert D. Stuart, ALO to the ROK unit, was at the battalion headquarters, about one kilometer from the LZ, when the attack first began. "At 2305 I called for flareships and at 2320 they arrived. The weather ceiling was five hundred feet that night and visibility was less than one mile. I launched a FAC but weather was so bad he couldn't see at all. My first three flareships were Spooks (AC-47s) and the fourth was a Moonshine (C-47 flareship) from Nha Trang." 34/

The small Allied Force put up a valiant defense while the tanks and artillery ripped the enemy ranks with continuous fire. At 0430 hours the next morning, after five hours of sustained heavy fighting, the enemy force withdrew, leaving behind 197 NVA bodies and six prisoners. Another prisoner, captured months later, revealed that the enemy battalion commander was among the dead that night. Friendly losses for the battle were seven Koreans KIA, 42 WIA, and three Americans WIA. 35/

Early in the afternoon on 10 August, a FAC directed two A-1Es on a close support mission for A/2/12th. Artillery and the TAC air strikes were credited with breaking off the enemy contact and the FAC estimated 15 KBA as a result of the strike. 36/

The Battalion Commander of 2/12th Cav made the following comment on this support: "On 10 Aug 66, the timely use of artillery followed by an ARA strike and FAC-directed close air support mission broke up NVA units attempting to encircle A/2/12 Cav and forced the NVA unit's heavy weapons to break contact and immediately withdraw. 37/ The Company Commander added "that the air strike was a vital factor in turning the NVA attack and allowing the friendly unit to exploit the attack." 38/

Through 12 August, there were no other significant contacts as the enemy attempted to disengage and withdraw across the border into Cambodia.

Search of Chu Pong and Border (13 - 21 Aug)

Action remained light on 13 August as B/1/5th Cav, while sweeping their area, discovered a large but unspecified number of enemy bodies in graves. A ground reconnaissance of a B-52 strike zone was conducted along the eastern bank of the Ia Drang River by 1/7th Cav, while other 2d Bde units teamed up to capture a group of 16 NVA. 39/ Two medevac missions were flown during the day in support of the 2d Bde by USAF "Husky" helicopters. 40/ In the 3d Bde sector, one NVA, believed KBA in an air strike, was discovered. 41/

"Spooky" 21 mission was airborne in the area that night, and at 2030 hours began expending his 16,500 rounds of minigun ammo against a target developed by B/1/5th Cav. The after action report indicated these results: "Interrogation of a prisoner captured by B/1/5th Cav later indicated that the NVA 7th Co, 6th Bn, 320th (32d) Regiment lost half the company as a result of this mission and that the 9th Company, 6th Bn, 320th Regiment lost one third of the company during the same mission." [42]

On 14 August, A/1/5th was following communications wire along a major trail, when they uncovered an NVA ambush and turned the tables on the enemy, killing one and capturing another. Pursuit of the fleeing enemy led the Americans into a well dug-in NVA Company. Two more companies of the 2d Brigade were immediately rushed to the scene in an attempt to trap the enemy force. One of them, B/2/5th, ran into another enemy company and air strikes were called in. Napalm was delivered to within 15 meters of friendly troops, and B/2/5th Cav reported that as a result of the strike "enemy automatic weapons have been silenced. The enemy was unable to resume the attack and prisoner reports later verified that they withdrew during the night." [43] More companies maneuvered into positions to block escape routes into Cambodia, and air and artillery pounded the enemy positions throughout the night. [44]

This series of engagements continued on 15 August, as the entire area around Hill 534, part of the Chu Pong Massif, was found to be heavily infested with fortifications and base camps. The 1/5th Cav maneuvered four companies against these fortifications, while 2/5th Cav attempted to seal off escape routes.

Commenting on the TAC air support he received that day, the Commander,

1st Battalion, 5th Cav stated: "On 15 Aug, C/1/5 Cav employed an immediate TAC air strike on a bunker position with which the company was heavily engaged. Napalm was employed within 10 meters of the friendly lines against an estimated company-sized NVA force. This killed many deployed NVA, neutralized two enemy bunkers, and relieved B/2/5 from intensive small arms fire." 45/

Twenty-five Combat Sky Spot sorties were expended during the day in a north-south line along the border in an effort to seal it off and prevent the enemy from escaping. Two other TAC air strikes were FAC-directed against enemy positions on the west side of the hill. 46/ In the 3d Bde area, ground forces found 15 enemy which had been killed by air strikes eight miles northeast of Chu Pong Mountain. 47/ The 2d Bde was supported by six C-123 sorties which airdropped critically needed artillery ammo under the direction of Air Force Pathfinders who parachuted into LZ Cat. 48/ And that night flareships kept the skies lighted for the ground forces until dawn. 49/

The following day, 1/5th Cav moved out and secured the summit of Hill 534. After two days of continuous pounding by air, artillery, and ground forces, the enemy finally fled across the border. There were 138 NVA bodies found in the area and an estimated 200 additional NVA were KIA and 250 WIA. Combat Sky Spot missions and Immediate air strikes continuously pounded escape routes during the day. 50/ During one of these strikes, a flight of F-4Cs from the 12th TFW caused a tremendous secondary explosion about 200 yards from the summit of Hill 534. 51/

In another action, a FAC located and put in two Immediate air strikes on a group of 35 NVA in the open which had earlier eluded elements of 1/9th Cav. There were no confirmed results but enemy casualties were estimated to be substantial. 52/

Air continued at a high sortie rate in support of PAUL REVERE II until its termination. Friendly units kept up sweeping operations, with only occasional contact with small groups of NVA stragglers.

The Recce Platoon from C/2/35th again got into trouble during the afternoon of 15 August. Capt. Bruce Hoon was called to the scene to relieve the pressure on this unit, pinned down by an estimated reinforced enemy platoon, some four miles west of Duc Co, along Highway 19. Captain Hoon put in an Eagle Flight of F-100s with 500-pound bombs and four napalms and then finished with 20-mm cannon passes. 53/

According to Captain Hoon: 54/

> "They came through with some of the best strafing I have ever seen over here...They came down and were strafing the right hand side of the road with 20mm. Some of the stray shells exploded in the center of the road, so you can see this couldn't have been more than about fifteen or twenty meters...from the friendly guys...The troops did not sweep through the area after the strike immediately--it was the next morning when they went through. They said they found no bodies but they did find several NVA helmets that were ripped and torn from 20mm cannon fire. Several bloody trails heading off towards the west were noted."

The last significant contact with the enemy was made on 17 August, by a CIDG Force. The estimated enemy battalion immediately broke contact and fled before the encounter could be exploited. 55/

PAUL REVERE II terminated at midnight on 25 August. The 2d Bde, 1st ACD returned to Camp Radcliff at An Khe and the 3d Bde, 1st ACD deployed to Phan Thiet to conduct Operation BYRD. The 3d Bde, 25th Div remained behind with the 1/7th Cav attached and immediately went into Operation PAUL REVERE III. 56/

Results of PAUL REVERE II

Total enemy losses as a result of PAUL REVERE II were estimated to be 2,000 casualties. A total of 861 enemy were confirmed KIA by body-count and an additional 574 were estimated KIA. Eighty-three North Vietnamese and 36 Viet Cong were taken prisoner with an additional 18 enemy listed as Chieu Hoi returnees. The enemy was further estimated to have suffered several hundred WIA, including some 250 estimated for 14 and 15 August alone. U.S. losses were 90 KIA, 389 WIA, and three MIA. Korean forces suffered seven KIA and 42 WIA. 57/

Summary of Air Support

USAF operations (Appendix I) were absolutely essential to the success of PAUL REVERE II. Between 1 - 4 August, a tactical emergency airlift transported the 1/7th Cav Task Force, the 3d Fire Support Element, and supporting artillery from Dak To to LZ Oasis with 32 C-130, 7 C-123, and 18 Army CV-2E sorties. Between 1845 hours on 2 August and 1440 hours on 3 August, a total of 39 C-130 sorties moved the 2d Bde Task Force from An Khe to Pleiku. Again on 15 August, 16 C-130 sorties assisted in the movement of several units in conjunction with the operation. 58/

Once in the field, Free World Military Armed Forces (FWMAF) received massive tactical air support. The 1st ACD alone was supported by 145 Immediate and 452 Preplanned sorties which dumped 397.7 tons of GP, 52.8 tons of napalm, 37.7 tons of frag bombs, 48 tons of rockets and 134 canisters of CBU on enemy positions. Strike sorties for the entire operation totaled 823, delivering 660 tons of ordnance on enemy positions. B-52s responded with three Preplanned and two Quick Run (Immediate) strikes with a total of 27 sorties flown and 486 tons of ordnance expended. 59/

Supply became an extremely critical factor in maintaining the troops and equipment in the field when Highway 19, between LZ Oasis and Duc Co SF Camp, became impassable to wheeled vehicles because of adverse weather conditions and tank traffic on the road.

> "An Air LOC (Line of Communication) was established on 11 August 1966 between Pleiku and Duc Co and remained in operation until the end of the operation, at which time the air LOC was turned over to the 3/25 for their resupply purposes. During Operation PAUL REVERE II, a total of 882 tons of cargo was delivered by the air LOC, requiring 63 C-130, 11 C-123, and 20 CV-2B sorties." 60/

Extensive use was also made of airdrop techniques to deliver critically needed supplies, particularly artillery ammunition, to relatively inaccessible locations. 61/

> "When the 2d Bde moved to LZ CAT..., resupply became difficult due to the distance between LZ CAT and OASIS

25

> (approximately 43 KM), and also because of the
> limited flying weather in the AO. In order to
> augment the organic resupply capability, USAF C-123
> aircraft airdropped 5000 rounds of 105mm ammunition
> and 500 rounds of 155mm at LZ CAT. Also, 300 rounds
> of 8 inch and 300 rounds of 175mm ammunition were
> airdropped at PLEI ME. Airdrops were conducted over
> a seven day period (12-18 August) and required 50
> C-123 sorties. Of the 6100 rounds of artillery air
> delivered, 135 rounds of 105mm, 9 rounds of 155mm, and
> 12 rounds of 175mm were damaged and unusable.
>
> "During the drops, five parachutes separated
> from their pallets prior to impact, fourteen para-
> chutes either failed to open or partially opened,
> and five pallets of 8 inch ammunition and five
> pallets of 155mm ammunition were delivered to the
> wrong LZ. Overall, the airdrops were considered to
> be responsive to the needs of the forward elements and
> saved valuable flying hours for organic aircraft. Air-
> drop of supplies in subsequent operations is planned."

The 2d Bde, 1st ACD experienced some coordination difficulties with the airdrop of these supplies and recommended certain improvements. 62/

Air Force "Husky" helicopters were called upon to fly three "Dustoff" medevac missions in support of the 2d Brigade. To satisfy Air Force regulations, these aircraft were required to be escorted by a FAC and fighters or Army gunships. The Brigade after action report had these remarks about that support:

> "'Husky' type Air Force helicopters based at Pleiku were
> requested and used on three occasions to effect emergency
> medevac in adverse weather and during hours of darkness.
> The response of the crews, their obvious desire to help,
> and the success of their missions were a welcome asset
> to this operation." 63/

Air Force psychological operations (PSY-OPS) also made a substantial contribution to PAUL REVERE II. The 5th Air Commando Squadron provided U-10 aircraft for small-scale leaflet drops and loudspeaker missions; C-47s were utilized for larger leaflet drops. "Successful combat action, to include the delivery of overwhelming supporting fires and TAC Air, succeeded in providing the requisite credibility to the Psy-Ops message, and influenced the enemy to take advantage of the opportunity to rally or surrender." [64/] The success of these operations was borne out on 19 August, when four NVA soldiers waved down a 2d Bde helicopter in the prescribed manner and turned themselves in with Chieu Hoi (returnee) passes. A total of 18 returnees were logged for the entire operation. [65/]

PAUL REVERE II began terminating on 22 August. Air Force airlift again stepped into the operation and played a major role in troop movements. Nineteen C-130 sorties assisted in moving the Korean Battalion from Duc Co to Pleiku between 20 - 22 August. On 25 August, elements of the 2d Brigade were airlifted to An Khe in 21 C-123 sorties.

Flying 46 C-123 sorties, TAC Emergency Airlift transported the 3d Brigade, including 975 passengers and 361 tons of cargo, to Phan Thiet. An additional 13 C-123 sorties on 26 August completed withdrawal of the 1st ACD from PAUL REVERE II operations. [66/]

CHAPTER III

OPERATION PAUL REVERE III
(26 August-17 October 1966)

3/25th Div Operations (27 Aug - 17 Oct)

By the time Operation PAUL REVERE II terminated on 25 August, the large NVA units had withdrawn across the Cambodian border, leaving behind only a few small detachments and stragglers. The 3d Bde, 25th Div, consisting of three battalions (1/14,1/35,2/35), continued to conduct patrols and sweep operations throughout the PAUL REVERE AO, but contact was light throughout, generally with groups of ten enemy or less. The 3d Bde operated mainly from Pleiku due west to the Cambodian border, throughout the Ia Drang River Valley, and near the border from positions northwest of Duc Co to south of the Chu Pong Mountains. Maneuvering battalions changed positions every few days during this period to avoid becoming a static target and to keep the enemy off balance. [1]

Through the end of August, 61 strike sorties were flown in support of PAUL REVERE III operations. Heavy emphasis was placed on Combat SKY SPOT with 42, or more than two-thirds of the total sorties flown, being that type. [2] Poor weather conditions and lack of significant ground contacts with the enemy were primary factors contributing to this distribution. The only Immediate sorties flown during this period were on 27 August, when three F-4Cs, two A-1Es, and two F-100s were brought in by FACs on a target that produced two enemy KBA by body-count and an estimated four KBA. [3]

Contact remained light and sporadic through September. There were 283 Direct Air Support (DAS) missions flown during the month--53 FAC directed and the rest Combat SKY SPOT. These strikes produced a BDA of 19 structures destroyed, nine others damaged, and four secondary explosions. [4/]

Operation 50 (11 - 17 Oct)

During late September and early October, enemy forces again began to move back across the border into Vietnam. This was preparation for a new offensive, beginning with an attack against Plei Djereng SF Camp. To confirm the location of a reported enemy troop concentration east of Plei Djereng, a team composed of two U.S. Special Forces Advisors', 120 CIDG Mike Forces, and one interpreter departed from Plei Djereng on 11 October to conduct patrol operations.

Operation 50, as this patrol was termed, made significant contacts with elements of a NVA Battalion on 14 through 16 October, producing intelligence that contributed to the initiation of PAUL REVERE IV. During Operation 50, three Arc Light strikes were carried out in the PAUL REVERE AO on 15 - 17 October. The evidence gained through these strikes of enemy presence in the area precipitated the inauguration of PAUL REVERE IV on 18 October. [5/]

On the afternoon of 14 October, the Special Forces Advisors and their Mike Force Company made contact four miles east of Plei Djereng with what were believed to be two companies of NVA. The friendly force (call sign Stantion Option Alpha) immediately requested air support. This request was quickly relayed to II DASC. Lt. Col. Orville O. Scroggin, III, II Corps ALO, took off in his O-1 at 1600 hours to provide air cover. Fifteen minutes later, he was over the target area and made radio contact with Stantion Option Alpha. [6]

The friendly unit was dug-in on a small ridge and had a Recce Platoon operating approximately 400 yards to the east. The enemy, located to the west, was firing into the Mike Force positions. Colonel Scroggin called for the friendlies to mark their position, but they experienced some initial confusion when two yellow smokes appeared. This was cleared up when the ground force informed him about the deployed Recce Platoon. [7]

Within ten minutes of his arrival over the target, Colonel Scroggin began directing the first two A-1Es, Thunder Flight, on the enemy positions. During the passes, the enemy defended with two heavy caliber automatic weapons from a ridge 800 meters east of their position. Meanwhile, Maj. James D. Hawkins, Sector FAC, had also arrived in the area and was orbiting his O-1 to the west. He began processing immediate requests for additional fighters and passing them on to Colonel Scroggin. [8]

The II Corps ALO put in a second flight of A-1Es, Hobo 01, around the perimeter of the Mike Force at 1640 hours. This strike caused the enemy to break contact and withdraw a short distance. Beginning at 1730 hours, two more A-1Es expended, against the two enemy automatic weapons positions, followed by three F-100s twenty minutes later. These two strikes were apparently effective as both guns ceased firing permanently. [9]

Major Hawkins took over control of the air operations at 1800 hours, when Colonel Scroggin departed for Plei Djereng. He put in Buzzard 31 Flight, three F-100s, using MK-82 bombs and CBU-12s, which completely suppressed the remaining ground fire. He then requested a flareship and "Spooky" 21 was soon over the area. Major Hawkins also requested that two flares be dropped over the target area, and then he made two low passes under the flares in an attempt to draw ground fire and locate the enemy positions. Enemy reaction was negative and the FAC returned to Pleiku at 2000 hours. 10/

Before daylight the next morning, Lt. John Syarto, another Corps FAC, took off from Pleiku to cover movement of the Mike Force up the ridge to the east of their night positions. When he arrived in the area, Lieutenant Syarto initiated an intensive visual reconnaissance of the area and drew moderate-to-heavy ground fire from the east of the friendly position at about 0800 hours. The FAC then directed Hobo 01, a flight of A-1Es he had been holding over the area, to expend its napalm, CBU, and 20-mm against the source of the ground fire. As the strike proceeded, the enemy ground fire dwindled but weather conditions began to deteriorate rapidly. By the time the strike finished, a good portion of the ridge top was under cloud cover. 11/

Major Hawkins relieved Lieutenant Syarto at 0845 hours and put in two A-1Hs with 220 frag bombs. The fighters followed their bombs with 20-mm and triggered a large secondary explosion with white smoke. This strike was conducted in weather so poor that about 60 percent of the ridge line was in clouds. 12/

Late that afternoon, Lt. Col. Charles V. Gibson was diverted to the same area in his O-1 when the Mike Force again came under attack by the same enemy unit. Two A-1Hs expended their munitions 200 meters east of the friendly positions to relieve some of the pressure. At this time, the ground force notified the FAC that they had two seriously wounded, a Special Forces trooper and a CIDG, and one CIDG KIA. Colonel Gibson requested an Air Force medevac helicopter, which picked up a Special Forces replacement at Plei Djereng, and then proceeded to the friendly position. 13/

> "Because of excessive gross weight, the helicopter orbited the area a short while to burn off fuel. Braving ground fire and turbulence, the pilot, Capt. John Kreiner, made repeated low passes searching for suitable approach. At the suggestion of 2nd Lt Duus, the patrol senior advisor, the wounded were lifted onto the highest rock and the helicopter pilot hovered just above the rock while the replacement got off and the wounded were loaded, at 1730. The rapid rescue of the wounded and their return to medical aid is credited with saving their lives. 14/

While Colonel Gibson directed the medevac, Major Hawkins arrived and began VR of the area for signs of enemy activity. Three F-100s arrived and were expended, followed by two more Hobos which were held high in orbit. Another enemy attack began at 1810 hours, so Colonel Gibson put in the A-1s CBU 150 meters to the south and east of the friendlies, and napalm between 50 and 100 meters to the south and southwest. The enemy replied with moderate ground fire which terminated, along with all ground contact, after the ordnance deliveries. The Hobos finished the mission by strafing the area with 20-mm just as darkness closed in and rain showers fell over the target area. 15/

Early the next morning, Captain Griffin was diverted from a Preplanned strike mission to support the exfiltration of the Mike Force. The friendly forces suspected that their withdrawal route was set up for an ambush, so Captain Griffin requested three flights of fighters. The first flight, two F-100s, drew light small arms fire when it expended between the Mike Force and the next check point along its route. Two more A-1Es arrived and were held as air cover while two F-4Cs expended on the hill north of the travel route. [16]

Lieutenant Syarto relieved Captain Griffin a short time later and his Hobo Flight expended ahead of the troops to clear their approach to the second check point. During a strafing pass, the A-1Es triggered one secondary explosion. An Army O-1E, Puffy 51, who was acting as an artillery observer, contacted Lieutenant Syarto at 1100 hours, and requested an air strike against several huts which he was unable to destroy with artillery. Two F-100s smashed the target and triggered a large secondary explosion, causing heavy black smoke for three hours. During the bomb runs, all aircraft were under moderate ground fire. [17]

A few minutes after 1200 hours, Major Hawkins relieved Lieutenant Syarto and continued aerial surveillance, until the Mike Force reported they were close enough to their base to be out of danger. [18]

Results of Operation 50

Results of the three days of patrol contact were ten NVA and one Viet Cong Montagnard confirmed KIA and several weapons captured. The friendly force lost one CIDG KIA, one CIDG WIA, and one U.S. Special Forces trooper WIA. In no instance was the area of an air strike searched by the harried ground forces, and therefore substantial numbers of enemy casualties were probably never counted.[19]

The U.S. Special Forces Advisors attributed the success of the operation to two factors: "The outstanding support provided by tactical air," and "the outstanding performance of duty by USAF and USAF Forward Air Controllers in providing immediate and continuous air support."[20]

The Air Force role in the success of Operation 50 was highly lauded in the after action report:[21]

> "Especially gratifying and more responsible for success than any other factor was the very rapid response with close air support. All the pilots who participated in the air support efforts did a highly professional job. Particularly to be commended is the helicopter crew piloted by Captain John Kreiner, who made repeated passes at a very difficult and dangerous LZ to pick up wounded. He finally did make the pick up and was responsible for saving the two lives."

Final Results Operation PAUL REVERE III

PAUL REVERE III cost the lives of two friendly soldiers and resulted in wounding 22 others. Against this the enemy lost 36 KIA, 20 were captured, 182 enemy suspects were detained, 15 individual weapons, and 10.9 tons of rice were captured.[22]

CHAPTER IV

OPERATION PAUL REVERE IV
(18 October–31 December 1966)

Enemy Buildup

By mid-October, the commitment of large FWMAF units was again necessary to counter a large buildup of NVA forces east of the border and block another attempt by the enemy to initiate a sustained offensive. There was considerable evidence that several NVA Regiments had moved east of their Cambodian base camps and again entered Vietnam. The primary objective was probably the Special Forces Camp at Plei Djereng, once more emphasizing the importance the enemy placed on eliminating these camps. [1]

Before PAUL REVERE IV terminated ten weeks later, friendly forces confirmed that elements of six NVA Regiments (32d, 33d, 66th, 88th, 95B, and 101C), had moved into Vietnam. It took six weeks of hard fighting and over 30 Arc Light strikes to once more send them retreating into Cambodia. From all indications, it appeared probable that total enemy casualties for their latest foray into South Vietnam, cost the enemy nearly 3,000 casualties or as many as one-third of the total forces deployed across the border. [2]

Deployment and Initial Contact (18 – 29 Oct)

Operation PAUL REVERE IV was officially initiated on 18 October 1966, with the 4th Division assuming OPCON of the 3/25th Div with supporting forces. It also deployed its 2d Brigade to the field to conduct operations in a sector of the AO. During this period (Phase One), four battalions conducted search-and-destroy operations in the mountainous areas north-northwest of Plei Djereng, while two more battalions launched security and patrol operations in the area between Duc Co and Plei Djereng. Arc Light strikes conducted from 15 through 17 October were also exploited during this period. 3/

The first contact with the enemy was made on 19 October by 1/14th Inf, which fought a short skirmish with an estimated enemy platoon southeast of Plei Djereng. Scattered contacts were reported with platoon-sized or smaller enemy elements through 20 October. On that date, an Immediate air strike was utilized to silence a clandestine radio station, and an AC-47 "Spooky" broke off an enemy mortar attack against the Plei Me SF Camp by directing 7.62 minigun fire into the suspected enemy mortar emplacements. 4/

The first serious enemy counter-effort occurred shortly after midnight on 27 October, when A/1/12th was hit by elements of the 5th Bn, 32d NVA Regt. When artillery and air strikes were called in against the attackers, they withdrew to the northwest, terminating two hours of hard fighting. Heavy air and artillery fires continued until daybreak on possible escape routes. The 2d Bde, 4th Inf Div Company suffered three WIA during the attack, while inflicting known losses of 21 NVA KIA and three captured. 5/

During the late afternoon of 27 October, two F-4Cs expended four MK-82 bombs and four 750-pound napalms on an estimated squad of NVA exchanging fire with elements of a battalion of the 3d Bde, 25th Div. Despite steady fire emanating from the American positions to cover the medevac, an NVA soldier succeeded in working his way up near the southeast perimeter and took careful aim with his 57-mm recoilless rifle. The shell made a direct hit and exploded against the side of the "Husky," sending the burning chopper plummeting to the ground. The three wounded men being evacuated were killed outright. The three Air Force crewmen were injured and trapped inside the wreckage. Army troopers scrambled desperately over the wreckage and succeeded in chopping free the pilot and co-pilot. Despite numerous attempts to cut the crew chief loose, he could not be freed, and burned to death when the flames ignited the fuel tanks and the wreckage became a fiery holocaust.[6/]

More than an hour later, the FAC, Capt. Edwin R. Maxim, flying front seat, and Capt. Myron Crow, in the back, directed another air strike approximately 800 meters west of the crash site, triggering one large secondary explosion and a smaller one. This was followed at five minutes after midnight by a further air strike which drew moderate small arms fire against the A-1Es and the FAC. It resulted in a damaged A-1E, but the pilot was able to complete the mission.[7/]

The total friendly losses for the night's action, including the helicopter crash, were seven KIA and eight WIA. The enemy left behind 19 KIA, 18 small arms, 99 rounds of 82-mm mortar ammo, and 40 B-40 antitank rounds.[8/]

In a separate action on the night of 28 August, an AC-47 carried out a strike and flare mission in support of another American element. A prisoner, taken a short time later, revealed that the hail of fire from miniguns decimated one company in this battalion. The exact number of casualties was unknown to the prisoner, since this information was kept secret in an effort to keep up morale. 9/

The next morning, the second USAF "Husky" helicopter, Pedro 57, returned to the chopper crash scene of the previous night and successfully evacuated the two injured crewmen. Pedro 56 then continued rescuing seriously wounded ground troops until he, in turn, was shot down late in the afternoon. The pilot successfully autorotated his craft to a landing near friendly troops without further damage. 10/

Ground contact remained heavy throughout the day, with B/2/8th and C/2/8th Inf experiencing separate early morning attacks by battalion-sized elements from the 33d NVA Regiment. In both cases, the enemy attempted to overrun the friendly positions by numerous standing assaults. The attack against B/2/8th cost the loss of another UH-1D ammo resupply helicopter, which was shot down and destroyed by enemy ground fire. 11/

C/2/35th Inf, the unit heavily assaulted the previous night, continued to make contact with small enemy units that day. Three strike missions supported these contacts and were credited with two secondary explosions and an estimated four KBA. That evening, an AC-47 broke off a mortar attack against 2/35th by its mere presence overhead.

The various battles and skirmishes on 29 August, cost ten Americans killed and 43 wounded. Enemy losses totaled 51 NVA KIA, confirmed by body-count, and three NVA captured. 12/

The Search Steps Up (30 Oct - 8 Nov)

Phase Two of PAUL REVERE IV lasted from 30 October to 2 December 1966; it was the most bitter fighting of the operation. The three-week interim from 28 October through 18 November, was the period of heaviest contact, during which the enemy sustained staggering losses, frustrated his latest offensive plans, and forced him to begin withdrawing once again across the Cambodian border. 13/

The 2d Brigade, 1st Air Cavalry Division arrived to reinforce the operation on 31 October, and took over the southern portion of the PAUL REVERE AO. This move greatly strengthened the search-and-destroy capability of the friendly forces, and freed the other two brigades to concentrate on the northern half of the AO, where the major enemy buildup was believed to have occurred. 14/ The effects of the large-scale sweeping operations and numerous B-52 strikes during this period had serious deleterious effects on the enemy's posture in the area as indicated by the after action report of the 4th Infantry Division. 15/

> "Enemy plans to attack Plei Djereng and to later destroy US reaction forces north and west of the Se San River were apparently disrupted by the pressure of US Forces and the continuous air and artillery strikes against his units. The enemy suffered heavy casualties during his engagements with US Forces and as a result of artillery, close air strikes, and B-52 activity. PW's indicated that the morale of their units was generally low because of heavy casualties, shortage of food and medicine, and a high incidence of disease. Withdrawal and redeployment into positions along the Cambodian border enabled the enemy to take advantage of the proximity of the border to mass his forces and fire power against advancing US Forces."

Phase Two of PAUL REVERE IV began with the 1/35th airlifting across the Se San River to fill the gap between the 2/35th Inf and 1/12th Inf. Air continued to heavily support the ground forces with Immediate and DAS sorties. In support of the 3d Bde, 25th Div alone, air strikes were credited with triggering two secondary explosions, destroying two enemy structures and a footbridge, damaging two other structures, and an estimated five enemy KBA. During the day, a UH-1D helicopter was shot down, killing all four crewmen aboard. [16]

Search-and-destroy operations continued with steady but relatively light contact through the first week of November, but when a Special Forces-advised Mike Force was inserted west of the Nam Sathay River on 8 November, several days of savage fighting erupted. [17]

Deployment Across Nam Sathay (8 - 10 Nov)

During the previous three months, considerable evidence was accumulated indicating that the area along the Cambodian border, west of the Nam Sathay River, was a major base area for the NVA. A large amount of heavy trail activity, base camps, new bunkers, and fortifications had been observed or reported in the area and air strikes had resulted in large numbers of secondary explosions. Consequently, when flood-swollen rivers subsided sufficiently to permit access and movement into and through the area, Operation PRONG was initiated. [18]

Twenty-five U.S. Special Forces and 365 CIDG Mike Forces were inserted into an LZ west of the Nam Sathay on 8 November, to commence search-and-destroy activities. All went well until the next day, when the Task Force made a total of five contacts with up to company-sized enemy elements.[19]

At midafternoon, Major Hawkins and Colonel Scroggin were diverted from VR missions in response to a call from the Task Force for immediate air support. The friendly force (call sign Soapy Cause) was in continuous contact and had taken moderate casualties. Colonel Scroggin put in a flight of two A-1Es, Hobo 02, which immediately caused the enemy to break contact. A second flight of Hobos was held in air cap while the CIDG element withdrew to a prepared LZ. The Hobo Flight was then diverted to another area to expend. This series of contacts produced a total of seven NVA KIA, four NVA captured with 12 days' rations, one box of 12.7 ammo, two 12.7-mm antiaircraft machine guns, three AE-47 assault rifles, and three grenades. The CIDG elements suffered two KIA and three WIA.[20]

Task Force PRONG again made contact at 1130 hours on 10 November. The enemy continued to engage for half an hour but withdrew at noon. More than two hours later, the battle again flared and a Corps FAC, Captain Partridge, was summoned to the scene. When Captain Partridge arrived, he learned that Soapy Cause was in contact and receiving moderate fire. The ground force tossed out smoke grenades and stated that they were being hit on the flank and had taken casualties. Two Army gunships had already made several strafing passes and artillery was scouring an area 600 meters to the southwest.[21] Then, according to the Task Force PRONG after action report:[22]

> "Capt Partridge made a pass over the marking smoke to positively identify the friendly position and picked

> up moderate automatic weapons fire. At this time the
> friendlies began to consolidate their position and
> move North (sic) and East (sic) of a trail which ran
> N.W. to S.E. Soapy Cause released a smoke to mark
> his new position and came under heavy attack. Since
> the enemy was hugging Soapy Cause on three sides, the
> gunships and artillery had little effect in suppressing
> the enemy fire. Soapy Cause could not withdraw further
> as the forth (sic) side was an open area in which he
> suspected an ambush had been set up. Soapy Cause
> requested immediate air support and stated that the
> enemy had a much larger force and the friendlies were
> in grave danger of being overrun."

Captain Partridge requested fighters at 1450 hours, which arrived within ten minutes. This divert flight was Castor, three VNAF A-1Es, which the FAC, himself under fire, immediately began to direct 50 meters south of the Mike Force. The three aircraft delivered five 500-pound bombs and sixteen 220-pound frag clusters as close as 30 meters from the CIDG lines with "fantastic accuracy." As the strike progressed, enemy fire gradually decreased. The FAC gave the departing fighters a BDA of three KBA, as he saw them sprawled around the bomb craters. 23/

Immediately thereafter, Captain Partridge began to put in flight Hobo 01 with 500 and 250-pound napalms and ten cans of CBU-14. 24/

> "He first put in two smokes placed parallel to the trail
> running NW to SE and about 50 meters SW of the friendly
> position. He directed the expenditure of CBU-14 as close
> to the friendlies as possible. The first pass was a little
> inside of the mark which made it more effective but too
> close to the friendlies. The next pass was right on target
> and all subsequent passes were gradually moved south and
> west to cover the area. Enemy contact started to break
> at this point with diminishing fire being directed at
> both the ground forces and the FAC." 25/

While this strike was in progress, Captain Partridge was relieved by Colonel Scroggin who, during the next 90 minutes, finished the strike and put in three more all around the besieged friendly force. In the meantime, Major Hawkins had also arrived overhead and began covering for the aerial assault of a company from 1/14th, the division reserve force assisting Task Force PRONG. 26/

While the air strikes were still in progress, reinforcements from A/1/14th Infantry began to land in a nearby LZ. Major Hawkins observed that these troops made no attempt to leave their LZ. He made several unsuccessful attempts to contact the newly-landed force by radio and tell them to move out to relieve the CIDG Force. When they failed to come up on his radio frequency, Major Hawkins made three low-level passes over the LZ trying to signal them to come up on frequency and move out to the south, but to no avail. He finally wrote a message on a large piece of map, giving his radio frequency and stating the urgent need for their assistance to the south. Then he dropped it over the LZ on an extremely low-level pass. Immediately thereafter, the company established radio communication and began moving out to the south, where they joined up with Task Force PRONG at 2240 hours. 27/

The day's action resulted in a bad mauling for Task Force PRONG, which suffered one USSF KIA, two USSF WIA, and heavy CIDG casualties. Confirmed enemy losses were eight NVA KIA and two POWs, but actual losses were undoubtedly much higher since most of the air strikes were never exploited by the hard-pressed ground forces. 28/

Task Force PRONG in Trouble (11 Nov)

The NVA again hit Task Force PRONG on 11 November. Another element of the Task Force, call sign Lone Slump, was in a position about four miles northwest of the previous day's contact and less than a thousand meters from the Cambodian border. Lone Slump consisted of two elements, Lone Slump Alpha, located on the east side of a small dried up lake bed, and Lone Slump Bravo, on the west side. At approximately 0700 hours on 11 November, Bravo element made contact with a large NVA Force and called for immediate air support.

Lieutenant Syarto, a Corps FAC, was overhead providing air cover and put in the request. At the same time, another FAC was requested as it appeared that two battles might develop--one on either side of the lake bed--since Alpha element was already beginning to receive sniper fire on its side. Immediately thereafter, both positions came under heavy automatic weapons fire. 29/

Bravo element was under such heavy attack that it was forced to abandon its positions and withdraw to Alpha's position. The enemy then initiated a heavy mortar barrage against the friendly forces, whose ammunition was beginning to run low. At this juncture, two A-1Es, Hobo 03, arrived and immediately expended napalm, CBU, and 20-mm fire on both sides of the Mike Forces. The enemy fought back with moderate fire against the expending aircraft, hitting one A-1E in the wing.

The Hobos were relieved at 0800 hours by an F-4C flight, Boxer 01, which worked over the same area with 500-pound bombs, napalm, and 20-mm. Each time the aircraft made a bomb run, the ground fire would die away as the enemy scurried for his holes, only to reappear and resume firing until another aircraft could begin its pass. 30/

Despite the heavy air support, the situation of the ground force had become extremely critical. The ground commander informed Lieutenant Syarto that he was in desperate need of reinforcements and ammo, having already experienced casualties of 50 percent and nearly exhausted his ammunition supply. Lieutenant Syarto passed the word to a 4th Division FAC, Cider 25, and Scrappy 56, an Army L-19 artillery observer, who immediately began to coordinate a resupply and reinforcement effort. 31/

Boxer 01 and 02 finished their last strafing pass and enemy contact was temporarily broken. Boxer 03 Flight arrived at 0850 hours but was held high for possible air cap of the resupply mission. In the meantime, Lieutenant Syarto, as a precautionary measure, cleared Scrappy 56 to register his artillery for use between air strikes. 32/

While the artillery was firing, the CIDG Force was again attacked from the north and south. The FAC immediately shut off the artillery and put in Boxer 03 on the enemy positions, again causing them to break contact. The remainder of the ordnance was then withheld for use during the resupply effort which was expected shortly. However, three more flights of A-1Es (Sipa, Hobo 03, and Thunder Flights), checked in with the FAC and were held in orbit over Plei Djereng. Since Lieutenant Syarto now had adequate air support on hand for cover of the resupply choppers, he went ahead and expended the 20-mm of Boxer 03 and they departed the area. 33/

The ammo supply chopper soon reached the LZ, but the moment it touched down, it was ripped by heavy automatic weapons fire which wounded both gunners and killed a USSF officer on board. The chopper immediately lifted off before any ammo could be unloaded. 34/

After the unsuccessful resupply, Lieutenant Syarto was relieved by Captain Twark who arrived in his O-1 at 0910 hours. Twenty minutes later, the enemy attacked from the west and was again suppressed when Captain Twark expended Sipa Flight on their positions. The enemy tried once more within 15 minutes, this time hitting from the west and southwest. He was again driven off by air strikes, this time by Thunder Flight. The results were only temporary, however, as 15 minutes later, the friendlies were again attacked out of the north. The enemy was beaten back on this occasion by Hobo 03 Flight, which pounded them mercilessly. 35/

All during the hour-long series of attacks, Lone Slump continued to plead for ammo, medical supplies, and reinforcements. Cider 25 finally arranged to bring in two more choppers, so Captain Twark held the 20-mm of the last Hobo Flight to cover them. When the helicopters reached the area at approximately 1030 hours, they were again driven off by heavy automatic weapons fire. The helicopters attempted to airdrop the supplies but they landed in the middle of the dry lake, out of reach of the pinned-down friendlies. The FAC put in the remaining ordnance of Hobo 03 in the tree line west of the Mike Force at the source of the ground fire. This strike produced two secondary explosions. Artillery was then brought in on the east and northeast.[36/]

Another Phan Rang F-100 Flight, Blade 01, arrived at 1110 hours and was held high for five minutes, while the FAC shut off the artillery. The F-100s then expended their munitions along the south and west perimeters followed by a strafe of the area along the east perimeter. The fighters completed their strike in 15 minutes and were credited with one secondary explosion.[37/]

Air continued to pour into the area throughout the morning. Captain Twark was relieved by Captain Griffin at 1140 hours, and Blade 03 arrived and expended on various sources of enemy fire all around the friendly perimeter. Ten minutes later, Major Hawkins arrived and, acting as radio relay, briefed the arriving flight of fighters, while Captain Griffin was controlling the prior flight's expending operations.

Using this method, a flight of A-1Es was put in to the east of Lone Slump and succeeded in suppressing all enemy fire from that location for the rest of the day. Blade 07 followed at 1315 hours to prep the LZ for the third attempt to resupply the ground force. After the strike by the two F-100s, Lone Slump stated that air had secured the LZ and that the helicopters could land. As the lead chopper went in, he encountered light ground fire which was suppressed by Hobo 07 Flight, permitting all three choppers to land, unload their cargo, and depart with the critically wounded.[38/]

Reinforcement (11 - 12 Nov)

Meanwhile, the 4th Division was preparing to air assault the 1st Battalion, 12th Infantry across the Nam Sathay to reinforce the badly mauled Task Force. B/1/12th was originally scheduled to land 600 meters northwest of Lone Slump, but when the last resupply effort succeeded, the troops were brought directly into the same LZ. At 1302 hours, the remainder of the battalion began to arrive by helicopter at an LZ some two miles to the northwest. [39]

Cider 22, with Maj. Elmer G. Alred and Capt. Roy L. Jones aboard, prepped the 1/12th (-) LZ with three F-100s just prior to the air assault. The landing went normally until one chopper passed over a field 500 meters west of the LZ and was blasted out of the sky. An accompanying helicopter wheeled around to take a look and was also shot down by concentrated fire, later estimated as nine 12.7-mm antiaircraft machine guns. The enemy had set up an elaborate ambush position, probably expecting that the fairly open field would be used as an LZ. Six 12.7-mm antiaircraft machine guns were located in pits in the northwest corner of the field, while additional guns were located in the tree line along the edge. [40]

When the two choppers went down, Cider 22 immediately moved over the area. Major Alred had seen the first chopper crash, and subsequently spotted the gun flashes as the second one was brought down. He had just been prepared to work a flight of F-100s which immediately moved over to hit the gun positions. However, an Army L-19 Head Hunter aircraft and another helicopter kept making low-level passes over the downed aircraft and prevented him from controlling the fighters.

The FAC contacted the Army Battalion Commander, hovering nearby in the Command and Control ship, and the helicopter was contacted and ordered out of the area. The L-19 could not be raised, however, and continued to obstruct the air strike, despite heavy enemy ground fire directed at his low-level passes over the downed helicopters. The Battalion Commander, cleared the strike, and Major Alred told the fighters to hit his smoke and disregard the L-19, since it would either leave or be blown up. The L-19 pilot finally got the message when the first bombs shook his aircraft and he immediately moved out of the way. 41/

While this strike progressed, Cider 27, Capt. Charles D. Henderson, arrived in the area and continued to orbit nearby for several minutes. When the F-100 Flight finished, Cider 27 assumed control of the air strikes and Cider 22 returned to Pleiku. 42/

Hobo 09, which had been holding to the south and observing the action, contacted Captain Henderson and informed him they had the enemy gun positions located and requested permission to hit them. However, a flight of F-4Cs (Boxer 01) had just arrived, and since these aircraft didn't have the fuel load to hold very long, the FAC decided to put them in first. Unfortunately, the number two man picked up a 12.7-mm hit on the first pass and both aircraft were forced to depart without expending. Cider 27 then cleared the A-1Es to hit the guns. 43/

As they lined up for their first run, Hobo Lead, Capt. Ronald Senac, later recalled that he swallowed a bit hard and wondered if he hadn't made the wrong decision--there were a lot of AA guns down there. The two A-1Es expended their napalm first and then followed with repeated CBU passes [44/] against the heavy ground fire which rose to meet them. According to Captain Henderson[45/]: "I tried to keep them as high as I could for as long as I could, in hopes that we would knock out most of the guns. The Hobos did a tremendous job of this..., I gave them, I believe, three of the guns in the bomb damage assessment."[46/]

As soon as the Hobos pulled off the target, the Command Control ship, with the Battalion Commander and the Airlift Commander aboard, approached the area of the downed helicopters and immediately came under fire. They banked their ship sharply to the left, while a helicopter gunship raced in to strike at the gun, but the enemy was ready and sent the chopper plummeting into the heavy jungle south of the field. To Captain Henderson, who watched it fall, "it looked like a sheet of flames as it went straight down. When it hit... it burst into flames rising twenty-five feet above the ground." At the time, the Army Battalion Commander remarked over the radio that there wasn't any use looking for survivors as there obviously weren't any.[47/]

Cider 27 continued to put in several more flights of air, with Major Hawkins, a Corps FAC, assisting in pinpointing the sources of fire.[48/]

> "I was putting in one flight right after another. They were almost coming at me too fast -- I had at one time three flights orbiting, waiting to get on, and with jets it becomes rather critical. I finally called back to the ground station

and asked that they hold off the flights until I call for some more because I did have too many. Flights were obviously being diverted from other areas and so they were arriving almost simultaneously.

"We were able to use all flights in the area and as the last strike pulled off, there was absolutely no more ground fire coming up at us, so I assumed that we got all the guns that were in that position."

When ground fire had ceased, Cider 27 swung his O-1 in very low over the field where the guns had been dug in. Below, he observed several NVA lying in bunkers around two of the destroyed AA guns.

Later that afternoon the Corps ALO, Colonel Scroggin, accompanied by Captain Reinhard, the 4th Division liaison officer, returned to the target area to search for further enemy activity. Their O1 did draw light ground fire and so Major Hawkins, who had also arrived in the vicinity, called for a strike. Blade 05 responded and was put in by Colonel Scroggin. Because of the near-darkness and low clouds moving in, the FAC marked the target by pinpointing it with his landing lights and firing the white phosphorous smoke rocket down the light beam. The fighters then followed the FAC in and effectively worked over the target. 49/

Major Hawkins remained in the area after dark and summoned to the area, an AC-47, which expended on suspected enemy positions. One secondary explosion was observed. The FAC returned to Pleiku at 2000 hours and the area remained quiet throughout the night. 50/

The day's action had been extremely costly to the friendly forces. Lone Slump had lost a total of one USSF KIA and seven WIA; 20 Mike Forces

KIA; and 40 WIA. Two UH-1Bs and one UH-1D had been shot down and destroyed resulting in 11 crewmen KIA and one WIA. The first resupply helicopter had been damaged by ground fire and suffered two KIA and one WIA. Another UH-1D was damaged by ground fire and one UH-1D was destroyed in an accident at Plei Djereng, in which two crew members were killed. [51]

Enemy body-count revealed only 30 NVA KIA and six NVA prisoners, all from the engagement with the Mike Force. A sweep of the combat area the next day produced 32 additional enemy bodies from the Mike Force battle. These losses probably represented a small fraction of the total number of enemy casualties for the action. [52]

The next morning, Capt. Miles G. Fisher, a 2d Bde, 4th Div FAC, while flying over the crash site where the third chopper had gone down the previous day, observed white marking material spread on the ground. An Army ground team, consisting of A/1/12th, soon reached the location and four badly injured crewmen were evacuated from the scene by Army helicopter. The ground team succeeded in reaching a second downed chopper from which they removed the remains of the crew. A 12.7-mm AA MG was also recovered from one of the destroyed gun positions. [53]

That same morning, a young helicopter gunner who had been aboard the first chopper to go down, succeeded in working his way to 1,000 meters from the crash location to the 1/12th LZ. While still in the air, the gunner had perceived that the helicopter was hit and going to crash. When the chopper hit the trees, he catapulted himself through the doorway. He later stated that several NVA stared up at him in amazement as he jumped into their midst. The enemy soldiers were apparently so astonished, that the gunner was able to scramble into the trees and thereafter successfully eluded pursuit. The other crew members were all killed in the crash and their chopper subsequently burned. [54]

It was not until 16 November that an Army ground team was able to reach the other downed chopper and remove the bodies of the four crewmen. It was then discovered that the helicopter had crashed on top of an NVA bunker. The bodies of three NVA and a case of 60-mm mortar ammo were found under and beside the wreckage. [55]

All Out Attack (12 - 13 Nov)

The 1/12th conducted sweeping operations and patrols from their newly established base camp throughout 12 November. In the LZ itself, S/Sgt. Frederick R. Schneider, Jr. carefully constructed a four-foot high sandbag wall around his radio jeep, which was parked beside a side entrance to the battalion Command Post (CP). Sergeant Schneider, with his radio and support trailer, had been airlifted into the LZ on 11 November, to set up the USAF Tactical Air Control Party (TACP). It was his responsibility to maintain constant contact with the airborne FAC and coordinate and relay any air support requests. [56]

Late that afternoon, Capt. Arlo P. Wendstrand had picked up the Sergeant's mail and airdropped it along with some cigarettes into the LZ. A few minutes later, Sergeant Schneider was sprawled across the seat of his jeep, reading a letter from his wife, when mortar rounds started going off. It was 1805 hours. 57/

At first, the radio operator was unconcerned, believing the explosions to be outgoing rounds. But as rounds continued to come in, he soon realized the camp was under attack. Tossing his letter on the floor of the jeep, Sergeant Schneider scooped four telephone microphones off their racks, and tumbled headlong into the small doorway in the sandbagged side of the sunken Command Post. "I immediately called for Capt. Wendstrand to come back. As soon as he said he was coming back, I called for air." The attack against the small LZ, which was to include up to 700 rounds of mortar and suspected artillery fire, had begun. 58/

When Captain Wendstrand returned, he and Capt. Roy Jones, who was riding the back seat of the O-1, began coordinating with the Army through the TACP in an attempt to locate the source of the mortar fire. Below the orbiting FAC, mortar rounds churned up the small, 200-meter diameter base camp and several fires had already begun to burn. Inside the perimeter, the 380 Americans tensed and awaited the ground assault, which they knew was imminent. 59/

1st Lt. James R. Thyng was lounging around the ready room of the Squadron Operations building of the 1st Air Commando Squadron at Pleiku. He had been standing alert that day and was due to be relieved in less than an hour. By 1807 hours, Sergeant Schneider's call for air support had been received and minutes later, Lieutenant Thyng and Maj. Berley O. Vandergrift, II, Hobo Lead, were airborne. 60/

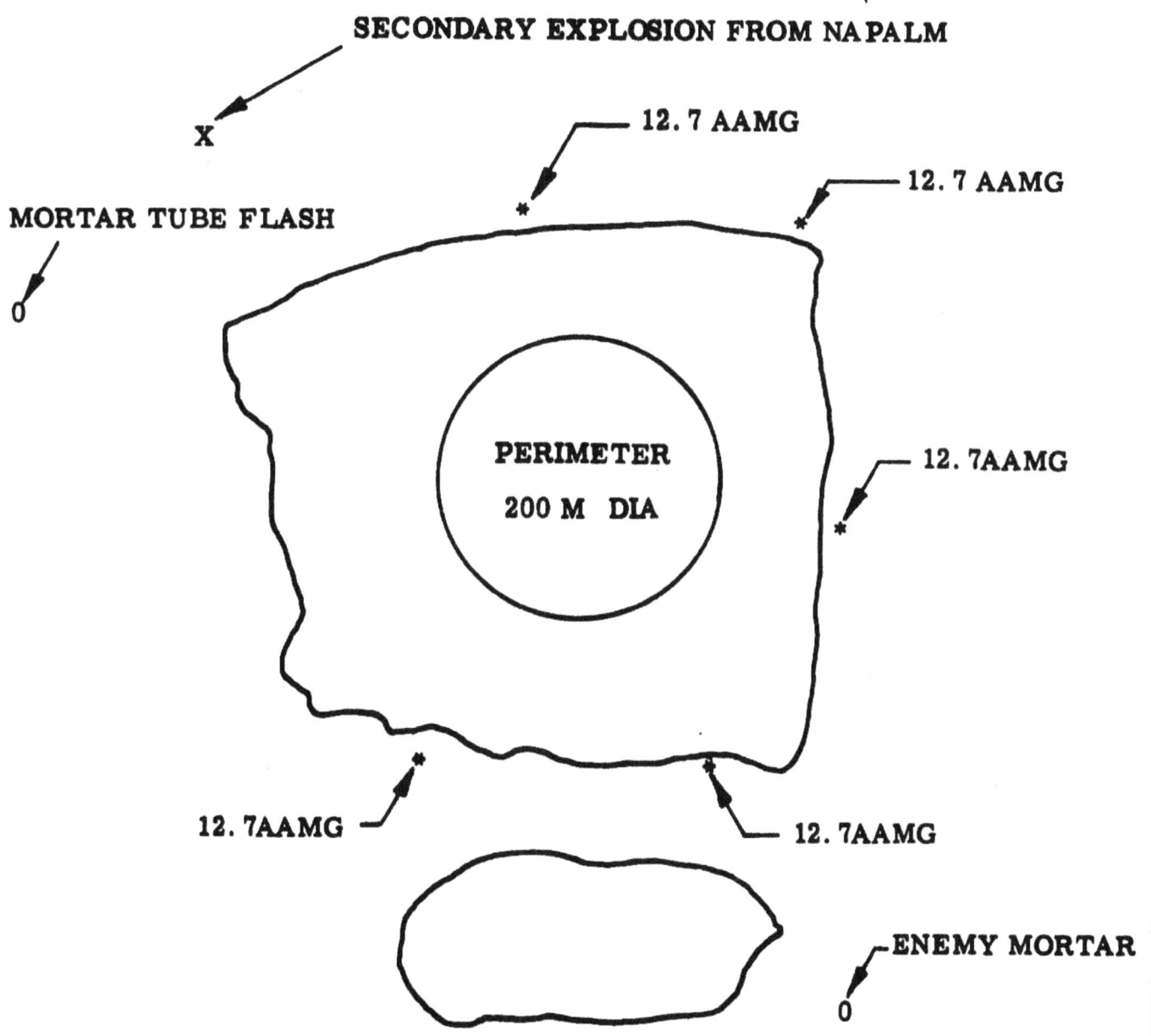

FIGURE 4

Once airborne, Lieutenant Thyng lined up on Major Vandergrift in combat trail and within ten minutes the two A-1s were nearing the target. [61] Lieutenant Thyng recalled his first impressions of the battle area this way: [62]

> "When we arrived on the scene, at fairly high altitude, the FAC... was Capt Wendstrand in the front seat...and Capt Jones in the back seat. Capt Jones was handling all the transmissions from the ground to the FAC and Capt Wendstrand was handling all the transmissions from the FAC to the fighter aircraft, which was ourselves.
>
> "From what I could see from the air in the last light, the terrain was fairly rolling and it was tree covered... As we circled the area, I was checking over my bomb switches, getting ready to partake in the attack, when my leader called out "They're firing at us, lights off! Climb five hundred feet!" Well I couldn't believe it, but sure enough, there were red golf balls flying all around my airplane."

As the two A-1s passed overhead at 8,000 feet, all five enemy 12.7-mm machine guns, carefully placed in a pentagon fashion around the LZ, opened up with everything they had, filling the sky with glowing strings of red and orange golf balls. Simultaneously, two battalions of the 88th NVA Regiment, some 1,000 men, stormed the north and west perimeters of the American camp in a human wave assault. [63] Lieutenant Thyng described it this way: [64]

> "All of the northern perimeter, extending around to the northwestern side of our troops was now solid NVA, who just about reached our perimeter. We then, Major Vandergrift and myself, had to make the decision...to leave the guns alone.
>
> "It had just become dark, and we did not have flare ship as yet to provide us light. We had our lights out, which complicated the situation because we couldn't even see each other, and the only altitude reference we had was Captain Wendstrand in his little O-1.
>
> "We asked him to turn on his lights and asked him his

> altitude. He turned on his red beacon and the wing
> lights and sure enough, he drew a bunch of fire..too;
> but he kept them on to give us an altitude reference..
> he was only at an altitude of around 1,500 feet, cir-
> cling the friendlies!"

Captain Wendstrand proceeded to mark the north and northwest perimeter with smoke rockets which proved unsatisfactory, due to the smoke from fires already burning in the LZ. However, when flare pots were ignited around the perimeter, the friendly position was adequately established for close support. 65/

Captain Vandergrift made the first pass with BLU-10 (napalm) but Capt. Paul A. Freeman, the S3, 1/12th, pleaded into the radio, "We need it closer. We need it closer." 66/ This time it was Lieutenant Thyng's turn: 67/

> "It was my pass--we decided to use mutual support, we had
> to cover each other--and during the course of the passes we
> came closer and closer to the perimeter, finally coming to
> thirty meters which was awful close considering the ord-
> nance we had was CBU and napalm....
>
> "We came in with our lights off and simply called out "off
> left" or "off right" to give each other an idea of where
> the other aircraft was so we wouldn't hit each other. As
> we'd come off the target, we'd immediately flip our lights
> on, drawing all the fire from the 12.7s ---and all the
> automatic weapons that the NVA were carrying during the
> attack seemed to coverge. All it was, was a bunch of white
> streaks all across the sky with all the 12.7 golf balls all
> around us.
>
> "I have to admit, it was a little scary at first until we
> got ... so involved that we couldn't pay any attention
> to them because of the closeness of our strikes. We
> had to put every effort in concentrating where we could
> lay down our ordnance, praying that we wouldn't kill our
> own men.
>
> "We could actually see what was going on as we flew over

and you'd pull up steeply as hard as we could without
taking off all your airspeed, just to get out of the area.
We did this as to provide an attack approximately every
forty seconds. We varied this so they wouldn't get the
exact timing down on us but we tried to put ordnance down
about every forty seconds. We did this for around thirty
minutes...before we were out of ordnance and out of ideas
and the relief finally came."

To the men on the ground, the Hobos screaming overhead every 40 seconds were a tremendous psychological boost. During the first hour of the attack, an estimated 500 rounds of mortar fire hit the camp. A single North Vietnamese soldier had managed to crawl through the perimeter and had thrown a satchel charge into the 105-mm ammo dump. As a result, for the next several hours, the camp was repeatedly rocked by fiery explosions from the detonating ammo. Ironically, the enemy soldier who penetrated the perimeter, managed to escape in the confusion. 68/

From the sandbagged doorway of the CP, Sergeant Schneider squatted beside the radio jeep and continued to give corrections and relay instructions for the air support. Suddenly he reported, "A loud explosion went off, and I saw a big ball of fire; dust flew all over the place, and the sandbags spilled in on the jeep. Then I decided it was time I got completely inside the three-foot thick walled CP." The next day Sergeant Schneider discovered that the mortar round, besides caving in the sandbag wall, had blown out a front tire and put 97 holes in the front of his jeep. 69/

The Hobos continued their strafe passes until all ordnance was expended. 70/

"We strafed out and still no relief had come. So we
decided the only thing we had left was to go in dry
hoping to keep them down. It seemed to work. We made
four or five passes apiece dry, hoping to keep them
distracted long enough that our own forces could

> revitalize themselves and at the same time wait for the support of more Hobos.
>
> "As we left the area, they were kind of happy on the ground. They were still under heavy contact. Nothing had changed as far as the NVA still being there and as far as the guns still firing but at least the immediate pressure of an overrun was off--which they claimed later was inevitable, if it hadn't been for us."

Another flight of Hobos finally arrived to relieve Hobo 01 and the FAC in turn had been replaced by Cider 40, Captain Fisher. He continued to put in air strikes for more than two hours, at which time he was replaced by Cider 27--Captain Henderson in the front seat and Captain Wargowski in the rear. [71]

Cider 27 was on target and being briefed by Captain Fisher on the ground situation by 2100 hours. Captain Henderson stated: [72]

> "In trying to get close to the target, we kept seeming to encounter the F-100s with their lights out, and in fact, on two occassions, (sic) had very near misses with them.
>
> "We had almost continuous strikes throughout the night except for a period of about two hours when the weather kept us out...I know at times we had F-100s, F-4s, A-1s... we worked a little bit of everything. We also had a Spooky flareship...we mainly used his flares but the guns as well. We concentrated them pretty much west of the battalion, along the border trying to seal off any escape routes the NVA might be using.
>
> "When we first arrived there...we could see the ammo dump on fire. At times, the ammo dump would subside and we could see the incoming mortar rounds as they would hit inside the perimeter...360 degrees around the perimeter and extending out maybe a thousand meters, every now and then we would catch the flash of one of these mortar tubes firing. Whenever we did, we would immediately put another strike on top of it. On one

of these...we did encounter a large secondary explosion...
so I'm sure we got that mortar tube, as well as some
ammunition they had stored in that area.

"We were working all around the perimeter of the battalion
as it appeared they were completely surrounded..The
friendlies were dug into their bunkers and we were able to
lay CBU right down along the perimeter without causing harm
to them, although I'm sure the fragments were hitting the
bunkers. The bombs we kept out just a little bit further,
but still the fragments were hitting inside the perimeter.
But that was welcomed by the friendly units--they didn't
complain at all on any of it.

"Some of the comments over the radio were that our ordnance was 'just right' and at times they could see the
NVA being burned with Napalm. It was that close in
proximity. I remember one company commander commenting
on a strike on the east side. He said, 'That's just
right, it's just perfect,' and he said, 'Please don't
bring it any closer.'"

Cider 27 was finally forced to abandon the area when a severe thunder-storm closed in. On the return trip to Pleiku, the O-1 got caught in the storm and the two pilots became temporarily lost. Their aircraft was nearly out of fuel and the carburetor began to ice up. When the engine began to cut out and they were still unsure of their position, the two pilots really became concerned. 73/

The radio compass wasn't functioning and Pleiku radar was unable to paint them, so when they didn't break out of the storm, Captain Henderson began to think they had flown west (the wrong direction), and that they were lost over Cambodia. Since neither pilot had a parachute, each began to make preparations for a crash landing, in the event the fuel became exhausted.

As a last measure, Captain Henderson again called Pleiku, and asked if they could give them a Direction Finder (DF) to bring them in. He was informed it wasn't operational at that time. Then Cider 27 got a call on VHF from Capt. Ronald Senac, informing them that he had an ADF fix on their position. Within minutes, Captain Senac pulled up behind them and gave positive directions to get to nearby Pleiku. The O-1 landed with a minimum of fuel. Captain Senac returned to the battle scene and started laying ordnance and directing "Spooky" on his own initiative until the new FAC arrived. 74/

Action continued sporadically throughout the night, but the main impetus of the attack had been shattered by airpower. When the first medevac arrived at 0730 hours the next day, the Fire Support Base again came under a light mortar attack, which lasted five to ten minutes before being silenced by counter mortar fire. At 0830 hours, the Battalion Commander, Lt. Col. James R. Lay, ordered a sweep of the perimeter, which again came under mortar fire a short time later. Direct fire from an 105-mm howitzer silenced this attack. 75/

Due to the threat of continued attacks and the exhausted condition of the American force, the unit was finally evacuated from the LZ at 1500 hours. Only a partial sweep of the battle area had been accomplished due to continuing enemy pressure, but within 15 meters of the perimeter, 76 enemy bodies were counted. A helicopter did fly very low over the area and the crew counted bodies visible among the trees and foliage. Four hundred additional enemy KIA were unofficially tallied in this manner.

The majority of these enemy casualties was the result of 77 close air support sorties flown during the night in support of the friendly forces. Two armed AC-47s also expended flares and miniguns and one other flareship mission was flown. FAC's reported a BDA of these secondary explosions. Friendly losses for the night totaled five U.S. KIA, and 41 WIA, six of them seriously. 76/

Especially high praise was given to the Air Force for their support of a ground engagement on the night of 12 - 13 November 1966. Capt. Paul E. Freeman, S3, 1/12th, in an interview the day after the battle, stated: 77/

> "Night before last I gained more respect for the Air Force than I've ever had...Let me talk for a minute about this aircraft they call the A-1 and known to the infantryman as the Hobo. This aircraft stayed with us continuously along with all of our FACs all through the night of the 12th and the morning and afternoon of the 13th; and there are many times that had it not been for this aircraft and CBU, we would've been hurt. And I can remember one time that we had at least half of our perimeter covered by Charlies and this A-1 ate them up in fine fashion. It's an excellent aircraft to use at night. The manueverability (sic) of this aircraft is just fantastic."

Lt. Col. James R. Lay, Commander, 1st Battalion, 12th Inf had these comments: 78/

> "I can say nothing but good things about the Air Force, particularly after our engagement on the night of the 12th of November...We used the Air Force in conjunction with our artillery fire all night. We used the Hobos and the high performance aircraft. In addition we used the C-47... and believe me, they did a tremendous job for us.. The FACs did a tremendous job in assisting us and bringing Close Air Support. I have nothing but the highest praise for the Air Force....

> "Before closing, there's one thing I'd like to comment on about the Air Force. In this past operation that we were on, I want to go on record as praising to the highest that I can, the Hobos. Now these aircraft, in my opinion, saved this battalion from many casualties. I particularly recommend to anybody engaged in this fighting to use CBU! Because the first flight that came in to support us, they had CBUs and at that time brought it in to within fifty meters of our perimeter. And I attribute our success in the initial phases of this thing to the effectiveness of the CBU and the Hobos."

The Search Continues (13 - 20 Nov)

Continued heavy enemy resistance west of the Nam Sathay River was encountered on the afternoon of 13 November. Three and a half miles south-southwest of the 1/12th LZ, A/1/14th fought a 45-minute battle with an enemy company beginning at noon. Later in the afternoon, the same unit was engaged by (an estimated) two enemy companies in a fierce 90-minute battle, in which the enemy troops closed to within 15 meters of the friendly element. When "C" Company finally joined up, the attack fell off, but not before 15 U.S. soldiers were KIA and 38 WIA. Known enemy losses amounted to 35 NVA KIA. 79/

On 14 November, Task Force PRONG was airlifted to Plei Djereng, while a Mike Force and a CIDG Company were airlifted from Pleiku to Plei Me to replace the battered Task Force which had suffered more than 25 percent casualties in three days of fighting. 80/

On 17 November, another enemy company-sized force was fought by A/2/8th and a CIDG Company, one mile southwest of the battalion LZ. The known enemy loss for the series of contacts was only one NVA captured, while U.S. forces lost one KIA and ten WIA. 81/

The following day, 1/12th found 12 dead NVA and their weapons in a B-52 strike zone. They estimated this was the result of an Arc Light strike on 5 November. At the same time, B/1/22d discovered a major enemy base camp on the west bank of the Nam Sathay and about three miles northeast of the 2/8th LZ. After an air strike on the fortifications, a bloody trail was found leading away from the area. 82/

Elements of 1/14th discovered a large 208-bunker enemy complex on 18 November. The next day, B/2/35th was brought in to reinforce them, freeing the 1/14th, along with the Plei Me CIDG Company, to sweep the area of the bunker complex and destroy the fortifications. Just after noon on 18 November, the 360 friendly troops were ambushed by two battalions of the 33d NVA Regiment, as they moved on the bunker complex. The friendly forces fought back for three hours but finally made an orderly withdrawal to an LZ. During the battle, the enemy positions were pounded by four air strikes, 1,900 rounds of artillery, and 300 mortar rounds. The enemy force suffered confirmed losses of 166 NVA KIA and one captured, while inflicting 19 U.S. KIA, 47 U.S. WIA, three CIDG WIA, and two U.S. Special Forces Advisors WIA. 83/

Arc Light Routes the Enemy (20 - 24 Nov)

At this stage of the operation, extensive Arc Light coverage of the area west of the Nam Sathay River was planned. As a result of several days of almost continuous heavy contact, two and possibly three NVA Regiments, were located west of the river.[84] According to the 4th Inf Div after action report:[85]

> "On the 20th, 23rd, and 24th of November, five separate but coordinated strikes went in the southwest part of this sector. The effectiveness of the strikes can best be judged by the fact that after the strikes the 4th Infantry Division units moved into the area with little or no opposition. The area which had previously been a strong defensive position with bunkers, tunnels and foxholes was now practically devastated. Innumerable bunkers and gun positions were completely destroyed. It was obvious that enemy personnel had been in the area during the strikes and had undoubtedly suffered many casualties, although he had removed the killed and wounded. In one area a cave was discovered with an estimated 50 bodies buried inside. Although not definitely established, these enemy dead were probably the result of one or more of the B-52 strikes."

In another section of this report, mention was made of an intelligence report which indicated that "one night during this period 353 NVA bodies were buried in Cambodia." It was further stated that "Four captives interrogated subsequent to the B-52 strikes claimed that the losses sustained by the 33d Regiment (to the B-52s) resulted in its deactivation and reassignment of its personnel as replacements to other units."[86]

During the same period, several other Arc Light missions were flown in the northern portion of the AO in support of the 3d Brigade Task Force, 25th Infantry Division. "Information from POW's indicated these strikes were successful in inflicting casualties, forcing constant movement, and lowering the morale of the enemy force."[87]

Contact Continues (20 - 21 Nov)

B/1/35th made moderate contact with an estimated reinforced enemy platoon on 20 November. Air strikes and artillery on enemy machine gun bunkers and automatic weapons positions finally broke the attack, and "A" Company withdrew to an LZ where it was reinforced by "B" Company. U.S. casualties were 5 KIA and 17 WIA against confirmed enemy losses of 25 KIA and four automatic weapons captured. In another quarter of the AO, on the same day, 2/8th discovered a training area and training aids for the 12.7-mm antiaircraft MG. 88/

There was only light contact reported in the northern portion of the AO on 21 November. While sweeping the area of an Arc Light strike flown the previous day, 2/35th discovered the bodies of 14 NVA in a grave. 89/

Enemy Attack in the South (21 Nov)

Twenty-five miles to the southeast, the 2d Brigade, 1st Air Cavalry Division was in deep trouble. Two platoons of C/1/5th Cav had been sweeping a heavily jungled area only a few hundred meters east of the Cambodian border when one platoon was ambushed and annihilated within four minutes by an estimated battalion of the 101C NVA Regiment. The last word heard from the unit was a radio transmission that the platoon leader was dead, the enemy was in hand grenade range, and they were marking with smoke for an artillery mission against their own position. At about the same time, the second platoon nearby was also hit by a large enemy force and received heavy casualties. 90/

Rash 27, Capt. Earl C. Mizell, had been diverted to the scene, when the first call for help came in. In less than ten minutes, he was overhead, sizing up the situation for the A-1Es he had requested to be scrambled from Pleiku. In the meantime, ARA helicopters and artillery were put in as a temporary measure until air support could arrive. 91/

Hobo 03 Flight was airborne with CBU and napalm three minutes after the scramble call was received from DASC Alpha. Thirty minutes later, the flight reached the target where the friendly platoon was locked in fierce battle with several hundred NVA and was on the verge of being overrun. The ground commander quickly explained the main direction of the attack to Rash 27 and then marked his positions with smoke. The O-1 then rolled in and marked with a White Phosphorous rocket for the fighters. Because of a strong surface wind, Captain Mizell experienced some difficulty pinpointing the target with smoke. The fighters started the napalm out a short distance from the friendly lines and gradually worked it to within less than 50 meters of the friendly perimeter. 92/ Captain Mizell recounted the situation this way: 93/

> "As we moved it in, we hit a point at which the commander on the ground sounded very elated and he stated that was where we needed to put the ordnance and it was having a good effect and to continue. We were putting in napalm and CBU in this position he marked as a good place to put it in, but he advised us not to put it any closer. Almost immediately he commented that this had broken the attack, that he could see the enemy, who were NVA, breaking off the attack-- retreating. There was a comment that he observed forty or fifty NVA running off a particular little hill...which commanded their positions."

After the FAC had expended the munitions of the A-1s, including their 20-mm cannon, he then brought in a scramble flight of F4Cs, Boxer 05, which was orbiting nearby observing the strikes. By this time, the ground commander related that the attack had been broken and that pressure was off his platoon. Captain Mizell therefore expended the F-4s napalm on the area where several of the ground troops had seen the enemy force retreating in their attempt to escape the air strikes. After the F-4s had expended all underslung ordnance, the flight finished with 20-mm. [94/]

According to Captain Mizell: [95/]

> "By the time the F-4s departed, all contact had been broken in the battle area. The comment was made...by the battalion commander who was in a helicopter and who held to one side and observed the airstrikes, that forty to fifty NVA had been observed as KIAs as a result of the napalm on the little hill which was extremely close to the front lines of the battle. By this time I was getting low on fuel--had been airborne for quite a while. There was another FAC in the area to relieve me on station and I departed the area. Later I was told by the ALO that the Army Commander...expressed that I should be told that the Air Force had done a good job and in all probability we had saved his second platoon...from being wiped out...."

The enemy had succeeded in wiping out an entire platoon, with the exception of one WIA, who had played dead. The second platoon suffered heavy casualties also. A total of 34 Americans had been KIA and 13 WIA. Airpower, however, dealt the attackers a hard revenge: An enemy body-count during the next few days brought confirmed enemy losses to 142 KIA--85 of which were attributed to two air strikes. [96/]

After this battle, all surviving participants were assembled, (including Captain Mizell) by Gen. S. L. A. Marshall (Retired), in an attempt to determine exactly what had happened. From the testimony of survivors, it was conclusively established that when the napalm first hit the enemy front lines, the NVA attack disintegrated and numerous American survivors had witnessed NVA running from the strikes, some of them on fire. 97/

Captain Mizell recalled that "several of the survivors who were there, stated that they had seen enemy troops on fire, burning with napalm" and one Sergeant replied, "Yes, sir, there were people burning there. As a matter of fact, one came running out and was on fire and I had to shoot him three times before he died." 98/ In another instance: 99/

> "One of the officers who was in charge of the detail to police and secure the area in the days following the attack, commented that he was quite surprised to find nineteen NVA KIAs approximately three to four hundred meters from where the actual battle had been fought. And he stated that they were found right on the edge of a napalm hit. In his opinion, it was an obvious napalm splash...."

Final Phases (22 Nov - 31 Dec)

After the major contact on 21 November, there was only light contact with the enemy for several days. In sweeping a B-52 strike zone on 24 November, 1/14th discovered 50 NVA bodies in a cave and 16 other bodies throughout the surrounding area. All were believed killed by the Arc Light strike. 100/

1/35th Inf contacted an estimated NVA company on 28 November, and in sporadic fighting, killed 16 NVA, with losses to themselves of two KIA and one WIA. The last significant contact of PAUL REVERE IV occurred on

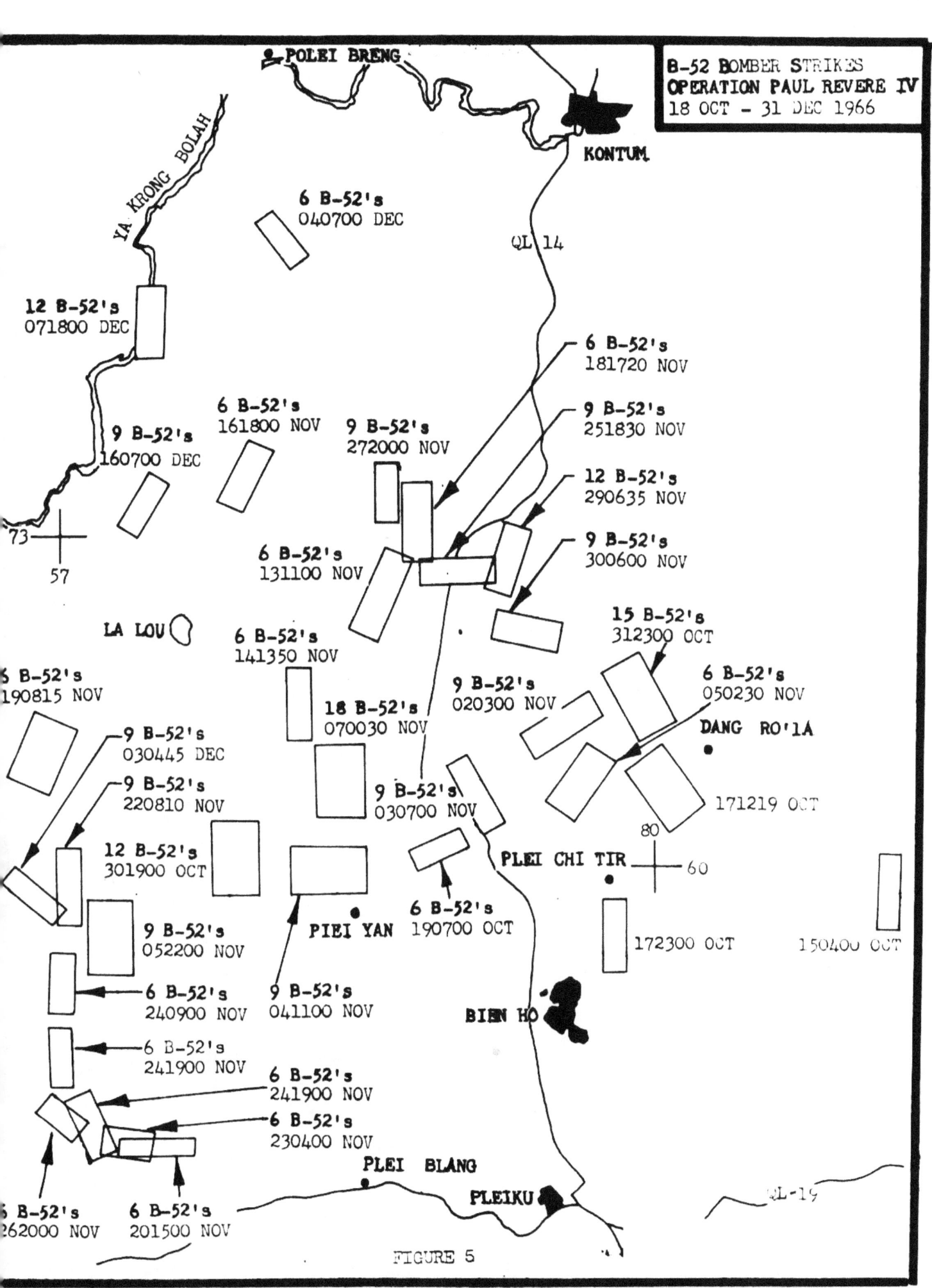

FIGURE 5

2 December, when A/1/12 made contact with an estimated enemy company, while on a sweep to the west of the Battalion Fire Support Base. "B" Company moved to link up, and an hour after the attack began, the airborne FAC put in an air strike 150 meters in front of "A" Company position. The combined American force then maneuvered against the enemy positions.

After a second air strike in close support, contact fell off and the enemy apparently withdrew. Three more flights of tactical fighters were expended on probable enemy escape routes, while the friendly force swept the battle area, discovering the bodies of 14 dead NVA. The two companies suffered casualties of four KIA and 14 WIA. 101/

Phase Three of PAUL REVERE IV commenced on 3 December, but engagements were only light and sporadic, as the operation was concentrated in the northern portion of the AO in an effort to contact and block the fleeing NVA units. 102/

On 16 December, the final phase of PAUL REVERE IV was initiated. During this period, extensive support was received from CIDG and ARVN Forces. Task Force GARRET, composed of a security platoon and CIDG Company from Duc Co, conducted search-and-destroy operations east of Plei Djereng. Concurrently, two ARVN Ranger Battalions moved to Plei Djereng and began search-and-destroy operations south of the 3d Bde Task Force, 25th Infantry Division. 103/ The CIDG Task Force MRONG and ARVN Task Force LUAT established blocking positions east of the 3d Bde Task Force, 25th Infantry Division.

The final two weeks of PAUL REVERE IV continued with only very light contact, indicating that enemy forces had either been rendered ineffective or fled west into Cambodia. Large enemy base areas and supply depots, however, continued to be uncovered throughout December. The lack of enemy activity and the New Year truce period provided the logical termination point for PAUL REVERE IV. Accordingly, the operation was ended at midnight on 31 December, to be followed immediately by Operation SAM HOUSTON. [104]

PAUL REVERE IV Results

The eight American battalions participating in PAUL REVERE IV inflicted heavy losses on what were believed to be elements of six NVA Regiments, two separate battalions, and an artillery battalion. A total of 978 enemy were confirmed KIA and 90 were taken prisoner; there were 331 suspects detained, and 14 returnees (the latter, 4th Div only). American losses were 136 KIA and 465 WIA.

Operation PRONG, during short duration, confirmed 102 NVA as KIA, 7 known WIA, and 3 taken prisoner. Three USSF were KIA, and eleven WIA. The CIDG Mike Force lost 24 KIA, 71 WIA and 5 MIA. In both operations, the confirmed enemy losses were only a small portion of the estimated enemy casualties, which may have run as high as 3,000 or more. [105]

As this report clearly indicates, air was the most outstanding contributor to the success of PAUL REVERE IV/Operation PRONG. A total of 2,795 strike sorties supported PAUL REVERE IV (Appendix II). These were broken down into 1,347 FAC Preplanned, 645 FAC Immediate, 576 Preplanned Combat Sky Spot, 176 Immediate Combat Sky Spot, and 51 "Spooky" sorties.

Operation PRONG received an additional 43 strike sorties, almost entirely FAC Immediates. The PAUL REVERE IV sorties achieved a BDA of 268 huts, 228 bunkers, 39 AA/AW positions, and 51 secondary explosions for their tremendous air effort. The B-52's effort totaled 32 Arc Light strikes. 106/

CHAPTER V

OPERATION SAM HOUSTON
(1 January-5 April 1967)

Background

Operation PAUL REVERE IV was immediately followed by PAUL REVERE V, which was renamed SAM HOUSTON, on 18 January 1967, retroactive to 1 January 1967. The 2d Brigade, 4th Division continued responsibility for the operation with various armor and artillery units attached, along with units of the 3d Bde, 25th Division and CIDG Forces. 1/

The enemy had been so thoroughly defeated during the weeks of fighting in October and November 1966, that contact through the first six weeks of operations was extremely light. Through 14 February, friendly casualties and equipment losses had been almost solely the result of mining incidents and booby traps, with one U.S. KIA and 52 WIA. Enemy losses were eight KIA, one NVA and three VC captured, two returnees, and 136 suspects detained. Miscellaneous enemy equipment and a large quantity of rice were also destroyed or captured during this period. 2/

About 1 February 1967, and continuing for the next two weeks, visual reconnaissance by FACs, Army L-19s, and other helicopters indicated numerous signs of enemy activity in the vicinity of the Cambodian border, west of the Nam Sathay River. The heavy trail activity and new signs of digging and fortifying prompted an Arc Light strike in early February, only a couple of kilometers from the Cambodian border. 3/

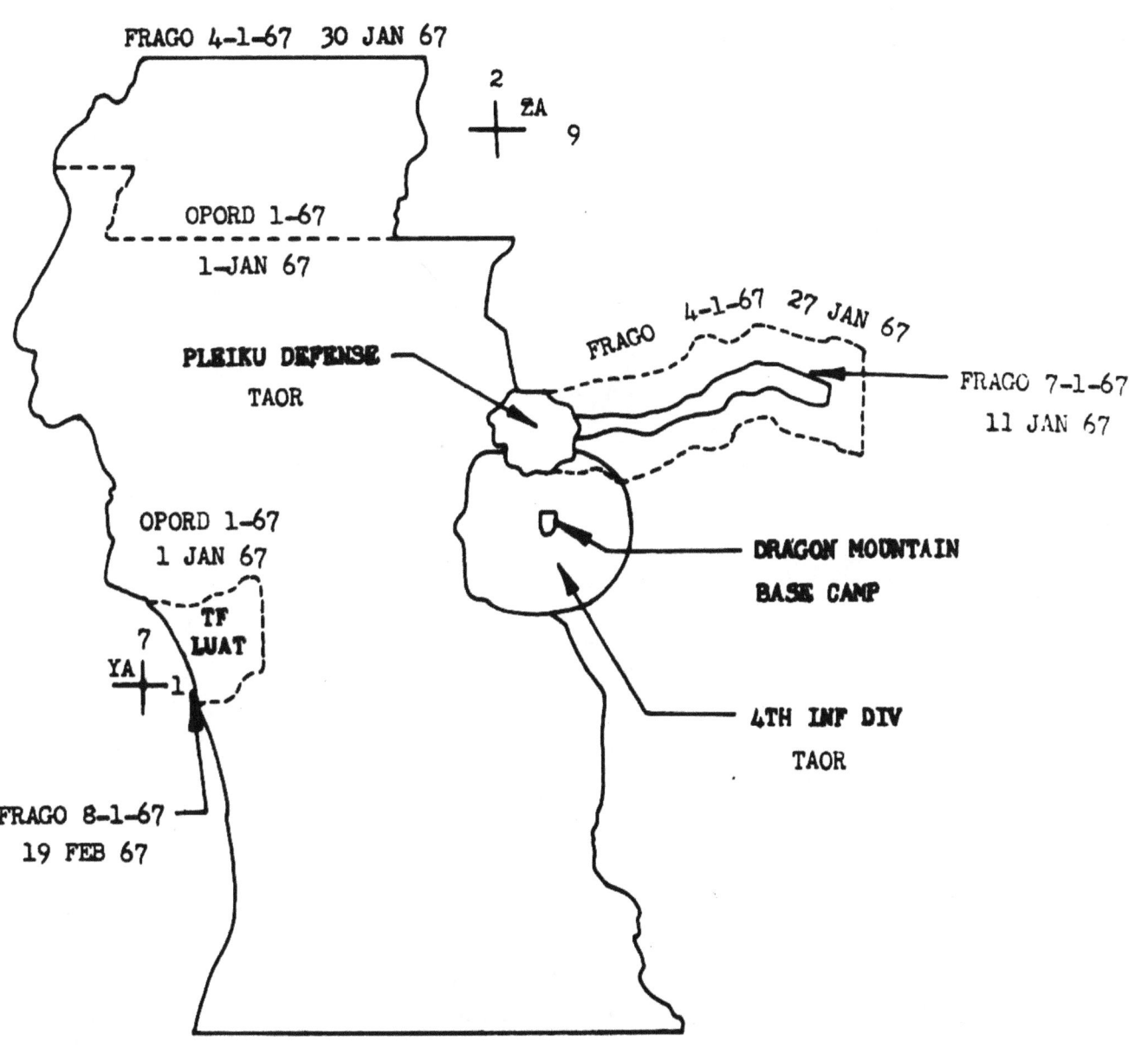

FIGURE 6

The Enemy Returns (14 - 18 Feb)

The 4th Division decided to investigate the activity in the area and made plans to send two battalions to search west of Nam Sathay. On 14 February, C/1/12th moved by foot to LZ 501N, where the rest of the battalion was scheduled to deploy the following day. The plan called for the company to search two hills that overlooked the LZ from the southeast and southwest. For some unknown reason, this was not done. The unit moved directly into the LZ and discovered it heavily fortified with enemy trenches and bunkers. 4/

This mistake in itself might not have caused serious difficulties, but on the following day when the rest of the battalion moved in, a decoy maneuver was employed and instead of prepping the actual LZ, air and artillery preps were targeted against a decoy LZ some two kilometers to the south. 5/

The night of 14 December, the Brigade Fire Support Base near Plei Djereng was hit by some 70 rounds of inaccurate mortar fire. Six men were slightly wounded in the attack. The enemy revealed his presence again early the next morning when LZ 501N was raked from the south and southwest by heavy mortar and small arms fire. The fire ceased after more than half an hour and the area remained quiet.

At 1334 hours, the first six choppers landed with elements of "B" Company. As the choppers departed from the LZ, the waiting NVA opened fire from the south and southwest with extremely heavy small arms and automatic weapons fire. Before the afternoon was over, two choppers were down in the LZ, due to battle damage, and 11 others had received hits. 6/

Air and artillery were immediately brought in to hit the enemy positions and during the next 24 hours, 42 Immediate tactical fighter sorties flew in support of the battle. 7/

Captain Henderson was the FAC when the first load of helicopters hit the LZ and his impressions were these: 8/

> "The LZ prep was changed somewhat to where all we worried about was supporting the company that was in there by themselves until we could get more choppers lifted into the area.
>
> "The company did sustain some losses right at first. There was a H-23 chopper that was damaged in the western side of the perimeter and automatic weapons fire started firing on any choppers that came near the area. The Company Commander, who was in charge, had pretty well pinpointed where this automatic weapon was located and obviously there must have been more than one, ...and so I controlled the strikes against this automatic weapons position which was in the southwest corner of the LZ.
>
> "We put 750-pound bombs in on the position and the company commander informed us that it was right where he wanted it. We were running CBU along the southern edge of the LZ and also along the western edge and dumped many cans of napalm along the west, south, and also concentrated on the southwest corner...It was then determined safe by the company commander to bring in a flight of choppers...
>
> "...The Company Commander told the S-3, who was up in a C and C chopper, to only let the...choppers bringing in the ground troops come in from the north, because they might still encounter fire from the west and southwest. Well, I observed the choppers come in from the west and I don't know what the slip up was there but the first chopper that came in got shot down right in the middle of the LZ....
>
> "We started putting flights in there on the 15th and we continued all the way up through the night of the 15th, and in fact until early in the morning of the 16th, hardly without stopping, except for one or two hours. At times we had as many as three flights holding, waiting to get on the target at one time...It was necessary the night of the 15th

A-1 COVERS LANDING ZONE
DURING OPERATION SAM HOUSTON
FIGURE 7

> to keep Spooky airborne pretty much all night and to
> keep a FAC airborne...with the exception of maybe one
> hour."

Capt. Noah E. Loy, another 2d Brigade FAC, was putting in strikes that afternoon in support of the 1/12th. At approximately 1500 hours, Cider 22, Captain Loy, put in a flight of F-100s which made dive bombing and strafing runs. While the strike was in progress, Hobo 01 Flight from Pleiku arrived. Captain Loy told the two pilots, Maj. Charles S. Kapsa and Maj. Charles E. Rodgers, to hold off and provide top cover in the event the Army was hit again. 9/

Immediately after the F-100 strike, the Army sent out a force to sweep the strike area but reported negative results. The Army then pulled back into the LZ and was struck from the same direction with automatic weapons and small arms. The FAC then ordered the Hobos to strike the area. 10/

Major Rodgers remembered the strike this way: 11/

> "At the time that we were orbiting, we were able to see
> ground fire in the trees and see the nuzzle flashes of
> the weapons. The FAC finally cleared us into the position.
> We concentrated on this area to the west of the Army LZ
> where most of this heavy fire was coming from.
>
> "Major Kapsa made several passes with his napalm, most of
> his passes dropping the cans in pairs...Major Kapsa was
> forced to deliver his napalm from a dive angle of approxi-
> mately twenty to twenty-five degrees. This is necessary
> in order to permit the napalm to penetrate down through
> the tree growth to the ground and strike the enemy posi-
> tions. If it was not delivered in this way, there is the
> possibility that the napalm can would be ignited and burst
> by the top of one of the trees and then it would spread over
> the top of the trees and burn up the foliage but it would
> never penetrate to the ground.

> "...And at the completion of Major Kapsa's strikes, they had us again hold off into another area as they went out and reconnoitered the area. The Army was still receiving ground fire from the area and it had not been sterilized yet so I then went into deliver my ordnance, CBU-14s....
>
> "I delivered my CBU in single passes to give us a long stay time on target and to provide better overall coverage by spreading it out over a larger area. I believe I made six passes in all...And at the completion of our passes we again climbed up to a higher altitude to stand by to support the Army personnel with our 20mm cannon. At the time though, there were other flights of fighters standing by to come in so they decided not to expend our 20mm and we departed the area to return to Pleiku to refuel and rearm, expecting fully for them to bring in another set of fighters to strike the area."

Captain Loy gave the two A-1s a preliminary BDA of five KBA (estimated). However, immediately after the strike, the Army moved out and swept the area again, reporting 42 NVA as confirmed killed by air. The Army estimated six additional KBA (based on enemy remains), nine bunkers, eight gun positions, and three automatic weapons positions also destroyed for the single air strike. [12/]

The enemy positions around the LZ were finally rooted out by continuous air strikes on 16 February. By this time, the mauling of the estimated two companies from the 8th Bn, 66th NVA regiment, left the battalion at 30 percent effectiveness. Confirmed NVA losses to this unit stood at 113 KIA and four captured; friendly losses to 1/12th were 12 KIA and 32 WIA. [13/]

The 2/8th and the 1/22d moved into new LZs in the same area on 15 and 16 February, and immediately fanned out to sweep their assigned areas. The C/2/8th was the first to make contact when they were ambushed around noon by

LANDING ZONE
WESTERN KONTUM PROVINCE
FIGURE 6

an estimated enemy battalion from the 32d NVA Regiment. Massive artillery and air strikes were employed in support of the ground forces and heavy contact continued until after dark. 14/

Captain Loy, with a new pilot, Captain Novack, in the front seat, took off at 1650 hours. Initially, the FAC was delayed in getting to the scene, because he was given the wrong coordinates by Alpha Seven Five. Then Captain Loy contacted Dipper One Niner, the Company Commander, to try and straighten things out. 15/ According to Captain Loy: 16/

> "This was the most frustrating thing because this guy was all excited and you couldn't talk to him at all. ...He just yelled at everything and all the trouble he was in. I was trying to find his position but he was completely under foliage and I couldn't see him. And so I asked him to send me up some flares but it took him three minutes to get a flare up above the canopy. Then I had him.
>
> "During this time I kept talking to him, trying to get him calmed down. And finally, after about ten minutes I got him calmed down enough to where he had confidence in me...and we got to where we could work together in a calm voice. From this time on, we started putting in airstrikes to the south of his position."

Captain Loy put in six air strikes for the 2/8th, moving them to within 50 meters of the friendly position. Darkness began to close in and the last strikes were put in under the flares. According to Captain Loy: 17/

> "I had to get a re-mark of his position with a flare because he continually moved to the north towards his (battalion) fire base.
>
> "After we put in a sixth flight, I had a seventh one and an eighth one in the area...while I was adjusting the flares, the Army got into a big argument on where the next airstrike ought to go, and at this time my two flights were running low on fuel. This was between

> Dipper One Seven, Dipper One Niner, and Dipper One Four. I interrupted them and said we didn't have time to argue and I couldn't move flares around on a moment's notice. It took quite a while to get the coordinates at night to the right place. And then Dipper One Niner got it cleared from One Four to put in another airstrike and about this time my two flights called, said they were out of fuel, and they had to go home. And so we put in some artillery in that area. After a while, Dipper One Niner said there wasn't any more contact and so I called off the artillery and stayed in the area until the new FAC showed up with Spooky."

The day's action cost C/2/8th heavy losses of 23 KIA and 21 WIA. One hundred fourteen enemy were confirmed KIA by body-count, but most of the strike areas were not swept until later, giving the enemy plenty of opportunity to remove additional casualties. The Army estimated an additional 200 enemy casualties from the air and artillery fires. [18]

That same afternoon at 1323 hours, as C/2/8th was fighting for its life, the A/1/22d, patrolling in its area, contacted five VC with negative results. About two hours later, the unit was ambushed by a well-camouflaged, dug-in NVA force and suffered heavy casualties. One platoon was almost decimated when the enemy mowed them down from treetop sniper positions.

Air and artillery were brought in and the enemy broke contact by 1700 hours. "A" Company then began to sweep the battle area but was again heavily engaged. Air strikes and artillery once more beat off the attack and "C" Company made a link-up at 1915 hours. Due to darkness, the battle area was not swept until the next day, but the enemy had removed most of his casualties and withdrawn. Losses for the contact were 20 U.S. KIA and 21 WIA. [19] Confirmed enemy casualties were 33 NVA KIA.

Another Arc Light strike, one of 11 in support of SAM HOUSTON during February, was put in on a target area near "Hairy Hill" on 16 February. Two H-23 helicopters from 1/10th Cav were scouting the area of the strike late the next afternoon when both were shot down and destroyed by heavy caliber automatic weapons fire.

The search for survivors was considerably hampered by intense ground fire from both sides of the Cambodian border. The FAC requested permission to suppress ground fire on the Cambodian side, but strikes were not put in. Several air strikes continued a few hundred meters from the border, but the heliborne reaction team was unable to set down because of darkness. [20]

The next morning the acting Brigade FAC, Capt. Eugene Fontinot, went up in the Command and Control chopper to direct air support of the crew recovery attempt. Air strikes with White Phosphorous were put in between the choppers and the border, only 600 meters away. This caused an effective smoke screen, while the ground team set down and worked its way to the downed choppers. One WIA was recovered from the first ship but a second man, who went off in search of water, was MIA. The two crew members of the second chopper were dead in the burned-out wreckage. [21]

Reinforcement and Search (17 Feb - 5 Apr)

From 19 - 21 February, a TAC airlift consisting of 75 C-130 sorties, moved the 1st Brigade 4th Division from Tuy Hoa to reinforce the 2d Brigade. Then for several days, the 2d Brigade searched the area west of the Nam Sathay, while the 1st Brigade took over an AO on the east side of the river. [22]

B/2/8th made heavy contact with an estimated NVA Battalion on 21 February, and had moderate losses of seven KIA and 34 WIA. Air was instrumental in beating off the attack and preventing further casualties to the American unit. Eleven NVA were confirmed KIA by body-count, 32 more were visually observed KIA but removed by the enemy, 30 others were estimated killed or wounded by ground action, and air and artillery fires were credited with inflicting additional estimated casualties of 75 - 100. [23/]

Action remained light-to-moderate, with almost no enemy contact, for the next three weeks. Then on 12 March, A/2/35 was hit by two battalions of NVA at midmorning. The contact continued until late in the afternoon and received heavy air support. [24/]

Captain Fontinot described the action: [25/]

> "They were in undergrowth and tall trees ranging up to 150 feet in height. Air support was requested and received in the late afternoon and ordnance was... placed on the outside of this area within 25 to 30 meters of the friendly forces. This relieved some of the pressure from the Army troops on the ground and they began to cut an LZ to extract their wounded... Another company was flown in before dark to relieve them and help maintain security around their perimeter.
>
> "The helicopters came under fire when they started going into the LZ that was hacked out. Air support was again requested and nighttime began to settle over the area. Spooky was brought in from Pleiku...Flares were dropped enabling the helicopters to proceed into their landing zone and deposit troops and resupply...Air support was continuously directed on all avenues of escape and around the LZ.
>
> "The ground forces were considerably hampered by not being able to get any artillery--it was right on top

> of a hill on a backside slope and anytime you have a
> terrain feature like that, to get precise artillery
> in is really hard. About the only way you can get it
> in is by air power.
>
> "The battalion commander had high praise for the Air
> Force for helping them throughout the night."

Late that afternoon, two more companies succeeded in reaching nearby positions to reinforce the badly cut-up American Company. The contact finally terminated after dark. The battle cost the U.S. 14 KIA and 46 WIA. Enemy losses that could be confirmed by body-count were 55 KIA. Probable casualties were much higher, with total enemy losses estimated at 200. [26]

Two days later, in the same general area east of the Nam Sathay River, A/1/22 was attacked by a large enemy force and also received heavy casualties.[27] Captain Fontinot again described the action:[28]

> "A patrol hit another unknown sized force and was just
> about wiped out...Hit them about two o'clock in the
> afternoon or so and they normally stop about three
> o'clock in the afternoon to start cutting away the LZ
> and set up a perimeter for nighttime operation. About
> this time they were hit so they couldn't set up a
> perimeter. They were in pretty bad shape...
>
> "Air was requested again. We struck air all through-
> out the area--again on the avenues of approach, escape--
> with CBU, napalm and high drag bombs. We also utilized
> Spooky again that night to light up the area. The
> helicopters did fantastic work and they were given
> high praise. I was directing on that one from 11
> o'clock at night until one o'clock in the morning, and
> boy that Company Commander had all praises for the Air
> Force for helping them out."

Results from this encounter were 16 U.S. KIA, 30 U.S. WIA, and 29 NVA confirmed KIA by body-count. The enemy carried off an estimated 25 dead.[29]

The enemy continued to harass friendly forces with numerous mortar attacks on the nights of 11, 13 and 14 March. The Fire Support Base (FSB) of the 1/22d was mortared on the evening of 15 March, and Kontum City was hit by approximately 40 rounds of 82-mm at 0100 hours on 13 March. These two attacks resulted in only light casualties. 30/

Late on 13 March, the enemy launched three heavy mortar attacks. The first confronted the Headquarters, 2d Bde, 4th Div against Three Tango, about a mile from the Plei Djereng Special Forces Camp. Another attack occurred on the FSB of 2/35th, with 60 rounds of 82-mm expended. (Thirty additional rounds were expended there the next morning.) In the third attack, which was against the FSB of 1/22d, about 35 rounds were expended during three engagements.

Artillery, TAC air, and AC-47s supported these camps throughout the night and friendly casualties were fairly light. The hardest hit was the 2d Bde Base Camp which received up to 200 rounds in two attacks. A ground probe was also carried out against this position, resulting in two confirmed enemy KIA. The mortar attack wounded nearly 50 Americans and did extensive damage to the motor pool. 31/

The last major contact occurred on 21 and 22 March. C/2/35th walked into a murderous ambush by a NVA Company on 21 March. For two hours, the American unit was devastated by small arms, automatic weapons, and mortar fire. This battle cost "C" Company 22 KIA and 53 WIA. A sweep of the area the next morning disclosed 16 NVA bodies and 31 more were discovered in the same area on 24 March, in shallow graves or where their comrades had abandoned them.[32/]

Early in the morning on 22 March, "A" and "B" 1/8th initiated a search for a battalion Recondo Patrol which had lost radio contact for an extended period. Alpha Company had been moving only a short time in two columns when it was attacked from both flanks. "A direct hit from a mortar round or B-40 rocket round killed the Company Commander and artillery forward observer. With the resulting break in communication, effective, close-in artillery fires were not available. The company fought most of the engagement at close range from two separate perimeters."[33/] Air support was called in and the enemy was pounded until he broke contact and withdrew to the southwest, leaving 136 bodies from the 95B Regiment on the field. American losses were 27 killed and 48 wounded.[34/]

Results and Analysis of Operation SAM HOUSTON

Operation SAM HOUSTON terminated at 2400 hours on 5 April 1967, and Operation FRANCIS MARION immediately became effective in the same AO. U.S. forces suffered substantially higher casualties during SAM HOUSTON, compared to the earlier PAUL REVERE phases of the campaign. There were 172 U.S. KIA, 767 WIA, and one MIA. Additionally, 5 helicopters (The USMACV Daily SITREP for 5 April claimed 6 helicopters destroyed and 22 damaged.), and 4 trucks were destroyed, and 25 helicopters, 26 tanks, 9 armored personnel carriers, 15 trucks, 12 trailers, and 6 support vehicles were damaged.[35/]

On the other hand, enemy body-count losses declined by comparison. The

66th, 88th, 32d, and 95B NVA Regiments were all contacted and suffered substantial casualties during SAM HOUSTON. Two other regiments contacted during PAUL REVERE IV, the 33d and 101C, continued to be reported by agents and POWs as having been disbanded to provide replacement for other units, due to losses sustained by these two regiments during PAUL REVERE IV. The Communist Forces suffered a total of 733 killed by body-count (725 NVA and 8 VC). Eight NVA and nine VC were captured; two enemy were classified as Chieu Hoi returnees, and 92 Civil Defendants (Individuals involved in violations of civil laws—draft dodgers, terrorists, spies, etc.), were detained.

As with previous operations, these figures did not give an accurate picture of total enemy losses. Additional enemy casualties for SAM HOUSTON were estimated by the units in contact and agent reports, from five to nine hundred and may have run substantially higher.[36] The after action report explained:[37]

> "The difficult terrain and dense vegetation in the area of operations assisted the enemy in his efforts to evacuate casualties from the immediate areas of major contacts and made the friendly effort to search for and locate enemy casualties more difficult. The absence of landing zones or clearings, suitable for helicopter extraction of casualties, required units to cut clearings in the jungle immediately following contacts with the enemy so that the seriously wounded would be evacuated. At the same time the enemy was able to remove his own casualties from the battle area.
>
> "The proximity of the Cambodian Border to the sites of most of the major contacts and B-52 strike areas made it possible for the enemy to transport most of his casualties to his Cambodian safehaven for burial or medical treatment. Agent reports and prisoner reports described

several movements of numerous enemy casualties into Cambodia following contacts.

"The enemy consistently makes a determined, almost fanatical effort to recover his casualties from each contact. His preparations for such recovery and his demonstrated efforts and willingness to risk fresh casualties to police his dead and wounded have generally proven successful for him. Enemy battle orders for defense of landing zones and plans for attacks on FWMAF positions have invariably included emphasis on all NVA dead or wounded being evacuated."

During Operation SAM HOUSTON, the enemy made considerable changes in his tactics from those employed during PAUL REVERE operations. These changes apparently made a sizable contribution to the unfavorable decline in the friendly/enemy casualty ratio. [38]

Enemy attacks during PAUL REVERE IV were nearly always staged late in the afternoon or after dark against dug-in rifle positions or Fire Support Bases. Friendly units were always able to hold their perimeters against assault until supporting air and artillery fires could be applied to smash the attack. [39]

The SAM HOUSTON after action report stated: "In contrast during SAM HOUSTON the majority of contacts were made by rifle companies while conducting search and destroy operations. The enemy avoided ground attacks against units in prepared positions." [40]

Maj. Gen. W. R. Peers, Commanding General, 4th Inf Division, elaborated on this change in his introduction to the division's after action report. [41]

"His (the enemy's) favorite tactic involved a procedure of reporting movements back, and, at a time and location of

> his own choosing, attempting to engage a rifle company before
> supporting fires could be effectively employed. He would
> simultaneously attempt to surround the entire company and frag-
> ment it into smaller platoon sized pieces using his favorite
> weapons, mortars and large numbers of snipers in the trees.
> His mortars were countered with artillery and air and his
> snipers by small arms, automatic weapons and particularly the
> M-79 grenade launcher."

The extensive use of these methods of attack against moving American units, without the protection of prepared positions accounted for heavy friendly casualties in almost every major contact. [42/]

This change in tactics had important repercussions on the application of airpower--indicating an enemy's appreciation of the deadlines of Allied air support and an attempt to negate its effectiveness. Friendly units were usually attacked or ambushed while moving through heavy jungle. Often substantial friendly casualties were inflicted, particularly by snipers, before air and artillery could react. This tactic usually placed the friendly forces in extremely close proximity to enemy elements. This fact, plus the dense overhead cover, dispersed deployment of a moving U.S. force, and enemy efforts to fragment the friendly unit, made positive identification of friendly positions extremely difficult from the air--an absolute essential before close air support could be employed. Thus, close air support was considerably delayed at a time when it was most critically needed. Despite the impediments of the revised enemy assault tactic, it was evident that tactical close air support was instrumental in repelling every major enemy attack of Operation SAM HOUSTON.

The B-52 supported SAM HOUSTON with 31 strikes which dropped 3,567 tons

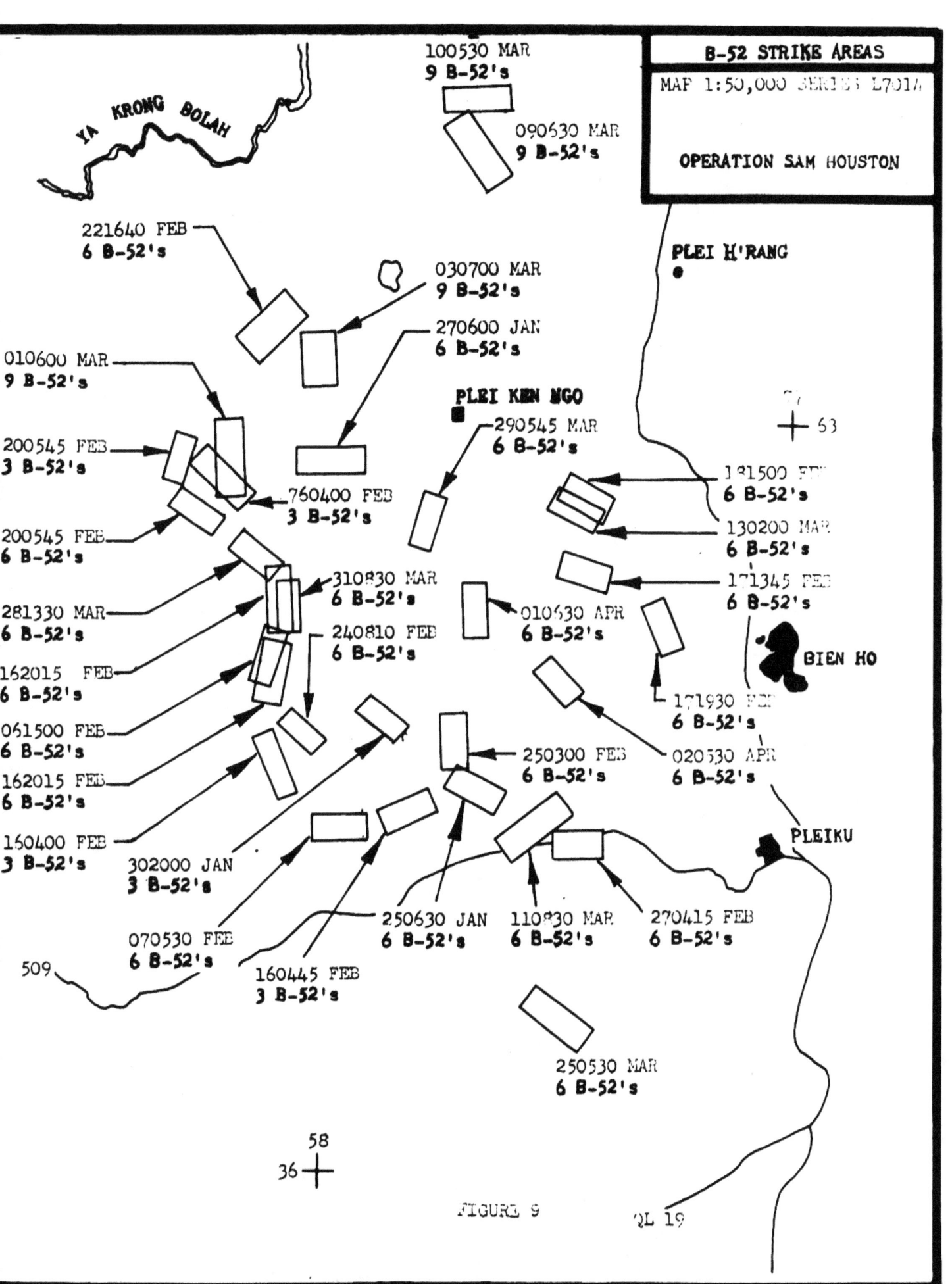

Figure 9

of ordnance on suspected enemy positions. No significant BDA was evident.[43/] This may have been, at least partly, due to another change in enemy tactics, which was an apparent effort to avoid the devastating effects of B-52 strikes such as occurred during PAUL REVERE IV.

In that operation, the enemy moved several regiments into large, well-defended base camps inside South Vietnam. This buildup was located by search-and-destroy operations and targeted to Arc Light. The enemy bases were subsequently struck and intelligence indicated that enemy casualties were in the hundreds. At least one regiment was reported disbanded due to losses from this series of Arc Light raids.

During Operation SAM HOUSTON, nine of the 11 battalion-sized contacts were less than 3,000 meters from friendly Fire Support Bases. According to the after action report: "It is reasonable to assume that the enemy is aware of the 3,000 meter minimum safety limit from friendly troops for the placement of B-52 strikes. Thus the enemy stays within 3,000 meters of a fire support base when he is east of the Cambodian border to avoid the effects of these strikes."[44/]

A thorough knowledge of the area by the enemy, enabled him to rely on small recce forces to pinpoint the locations of Free World Forces and monitor their movements. When a Free World unit was in a favorable position for an ambush or attack, the enemy moved the assault forces out of Cambodia over high speed trails, and into attack positions, in a matter of a few hours. Thus, large enemy troop concentrations were exposed in Arc Light-vulnerable areas for a minimum amount of time.[45/]

Although the chances of inflicting considerable physical damage to a major enemy force with Arc Light was probably considerably reduced, the continuing value of B-52 strikes in this AO was voiced in the after action report: 46/

> "The B-52 bombers provided another source of devastating firepower to the division...The raids were targeted on locations where intelligence indicated locations of enemy headquarters, base camps, units, and fortified areas. The psychological impact of the strikes on the enemy was one of the most important side effects. Enemy prisoners of war have indicated that B-52 bombers are a source of constant terror to them."

Air support (Appendix III) to Operation SAM HOUSTON totaled 2,500 sorties: 1,494 FAC Preplanned, 473 FAC Immediate, 409 Preplanned Combat Sky Spot, 57 Immediate Sky Spot, and 67 AC-47 "Spooky." 47/

> "Units continued to use the tremendous firepower and close-in targeting available from the fighter aircraft. CAS immediate requests supported practically every contact of the operation. Preplanned strikes were utilized by both brigades to strike known and suspected targets day and night throughout the AO. The use of preplanned strikes on targets developed by visual reconnaissance, recondo patrols and other intelligence gathering sources constituted the majority of the sorties flown." 48/

USAF tactical sorties delivered 8,152 bombs, 777 canisters of CBU, 3,396 cans of napalm, 477 rockets, 262,842 rounds of 20-mm cannon, and 310,000 rounds of 7.62-mm (AC-47s)--a total of 4,843 tons of ordnance. 49/ The 4th Division also employed the XM-27 Gravel Mine ordnance for the first time and reported the following results: 50/

> "This new self-sterilizing anti-personnel mine was sewn

> across the targets by A-1E aircraft. The type targets
> selected were fire support bases recently abandoned by
> friendly units because experience had shown that enemy
> units entered these shortly after the departure of the
> U.S. troops. A recondo patrol, inserted to observe one
> of the two FSB's on which mines had been placed, reported
> hearing several explosions during a 24 hour period. It is
> believed that the explosions were the result of enemy
> troops stepping on the mines. The overall effectiveness
> of the mines needs further evaluation."

The BDA from the SAM HOUSTON tactical air support included 176 huts, 322 bunkers, 20 AA/AW positions, 43 secondary explosions and 153 bodies believed KBA. [51/] Quoting from the after action report: [52/]

> "The damage assessment does not reflect the true value
> of the CAS used! This is especially true in the figures
> for enemy killed. Assessment of strike damage is often
> difficult to obtain because ground units sometimes do
> not enter the strike area until hours, or even days,
> after the strike, if at all. Strikes on the majority
> of targets must be assumed by aerial observers whose
> observation is limited because the heavy jungle frequent-
> ly prevents them from seeing the ground."

Conclusion

In almost every major engagement of the PAUL REVERE/SAM HOUSTON campaign, airpower proved to be an extremely decisive factor in the final outcome of the battle. It was obvious that the very survival of friendly units frequently depended upon the promptness, precision, and effectiveness of air support. Without it, the position of Allied Forces in the Western Highlands would have been untenable.

Airpower gave to the FWMAF the critical edge over an enemy who fought only on his own terms and was never enticed into battle unless he was thoroughly convinced of victory. Although friendly forces labored under this initial disadvantage, the record clearly shows that airpower was most often the decisive factor in balancing the scales to the friendly side and inflicting repeated costly defeats against a well-trained, well-equipped, and highly motivated enemy.

FOOTNOTES

CHAPTER I

1. (U) Notes by Lawrence J. Hickey fm Conference, 2d Bde, 4th Div Base Camp (Three Tango), 17 Feb 67.

2. (C) USMACV Monthly Evaluation (MONEVAL), May 66. (Hereafter cited: MACV MONEVAL.)

3. (C) Ibid.

4. (C) Combat Operations After Action Rpt, PAUL REVERE/HOOKER I, 2d Bde, 1st ACD, 9 Jul 66, Doc. 1. (Hereafter cited: PAUL REVERE/HOOKER I, AAR, 9 Jul 66.)

5. (C) After Action Rpt, PAUL REVERE, 22 Jun 66, Doc. 2. (Hearafter cited: PAUL REVERE, AAR, 22 Jun 66.)

6. (C) Weekly Air Intelligence Summary (WAIS), 7AF, 19 Jun 66. (Hereafter cited: WAIS.)

7. (U) Silver Star Citation, Capt Joseph A. Machowski, 30 May 66, Doc. 3.

8. (U) Ibid.

9. (U) Ibid.

10. (C) Interview w/Capt Bruce R. Hoon, FAC, 3d Bde, 25th Inf Div, by Lawrence J. Hickey, Binh Thuy AFB, 1 Jan 67, Doc. 4. (Hereafter cited: Interview with Capt Hoon.)

11. (C) WAIS, 11 Jun 66.

12. (C) Interview with Capt Hoon, Doc. 4.

13. (C) Ibid.

14. (C) Ibid.

15. (C) Ibid.

16. (C) Daily Air Activities Rpt, 7AF, 30 May 66. (Hereafter cited: 7AF DAAR.)

17. (C) Interview with Capt Hoon, Doc. 4.

18. (C) MACV MONEVAL, May 66.

19. (C) PAUL REVERE/HOOKER I, AAR, 9 Jul 66, Doc. 1.

20. (C) Ibid.

21. (C) PAUL REVERE, AAR, 22 Jun 66, Doc. 2.

22. (C) Ibid.

23. (C) Interview with Capt Hoon, Doc. 4.

24. (C) Ibid.

25. (C) Ibid.

26. (C) USMACV Daily Situation Report (SITREP), 24 Jun 66. (Hereafter cited: MACV SITREP.)

27. (U) DFC Citation, Capt Hubert E. Thornber, Jr., 15 Jul 66, Doc. 5.

28. (U) Ibid.

29. (U) Ibid.

30. (C) Combat Operations After Action Report, Operation PAUL REVERE II, 1st ACD, 25 Jan 67, Doc. 6. (Hereafter cited: PAUL REVERE II, AAR, 1st ACD, 25 Jan 67.)

31. (C) MACV MONEVAL, Dec 66.

32. (C) MACV SITREP, 31 Jul 66.

33. (C) Printout (IBM) on Arc Light Strikes, Working Paper, Undated. (FILE: CICV Targets.)

CHAPTER II

1. (C) Annex C to I Field Forces, Vietnam (IFFV) PERINTREP 7-67.
2. (C) Ibid.
3. (C) PAUL REVERE II, AAR, 1st ACD, 25 Jan 67, Doc. 6.
4. (C) Ibid.
5. (C) Ibid.
6. (C) USAF/VNAF OPREP/JOPREP 5, 1 Aug 66.
7. (C) PAUL REVERE II, AAR, 1st ACD, 25 Jan 67, Doc. 6.
8. (C) Ibid.
9. (C) Ibid.
10. (C) Ibid.
11. (C) Interview with Capt Hoon, Doc. 4.
12. (C) Ibid.
13. (C) Ibid.
14. (C) Ibid.
15. (C) PAUL REVERE II, AAR, 1st ACD, 25 Jan 67, Doc. 6.
16. (C) Interview with Capt Hoon, Doc. 4.
17. (C) Ibid.
18. (C) Ibid.
19. (U) Ltr, Capt Bruce Hoon to CO, 1st ACS, subj: Extraordinary Performance by Individuals, 18 Aug 66, Doc. 7.
20. (U) Ibid.
21. (C) Interview with Capt Hoon, Doc. 4.
22. (C) Ibid.
23. (C) Ibid.

24. (C) Interview with Capt Edwin R. Maxim, former FAC, 3d Bde, 25th Inf Div by Lawrence J. Hickey, Pleiku, 18 Feb 67, Doc. 8. (Hereafter cited: Interview with Capt Maxim.)

25. (U) Ltr, Capt Bruce Hoon to CO, 1st ACS, subj: Extraordinary Performance by Individuals, 18 Aug 66, Doc. 7.

26. (C) PAUL REVERE II, AAR, 1st ACD, 25 Jan 67, Doc. 6.

27. (C) Ibid.

28. (C) Ibid.

29. (C) Ibid.

30. (C) Ibid.

31. (U) Combat After Action Report, Operation PAUL REVERE I/II, 1st Sq, 9th Cav, 1st ACD, 28 Sep 66, Doc. 9.

32. (C) PAUL REVERE II, AAR, 1st ACD, 25 Jan 67, Doc. 6.

33. (C) Ibid.

34. (C) Interview with Maj Robert D. Stuart, ALO (Acting) CRID, by Lawrence J. Hickey, Tiger Town, 14 Jan 67.

35. (C) PAUL REVERE II, AAR, 1st ACD, 25 Jan 67, Doc. 6.

36. (C) Ibid.

37. (C) Combat Operations After Action Report, PAUL REVERE II, 2d Bde, 1st ACD, 5 Sep 66, Doc. 10. (Hereafter cited: PAUL REVERE II, AAR, 1st ACD, 5 Sep 66.)

38. (C) PAUL REVERE II, AAR, 1st ACD, 25 Jan 67, Doc. 6.

39. (C) PAUL REVERE II, AAR, 1st ACD, 5 Sep 66, Doc. 10.

40. (C) Ibid.

41. (U) Combat After Action Report, PAUL REVERE II, 3d BDE, 1st ACD, 5 Nov 66, Doc. 11. (Hereafter cited: PAUL REVERE II, AAR, 3d Bde, 1st ACD, 5 Nov 66.)

42. (C) PAUL REVERE II, AAR, 1st ACD, 5 Sep 66, Doc. 10.

43. (C) Ibid.

44. (C) PAUL REVERE II, AAR, 1st ACD, 25 Jan 67, Doc. 6.

45. (C) PAUL REVERE II, AAR, 1st ACD, 5 Sep 66, Doc. 10.
46. (C) Ibid.
47. (U) PAUL REVERE II, AAR, 3d Bde, 1st ACD, 5 Nov 66.
48. (C) PAUL REVERE II, AAR, 1st ACD, 5 Sep 66, Doc. 10.
49. (C) Ibid.
50. (C) PAUL REVERE II, AAR, 1st ACD, 25 Jan 67, Doc. 6.
51. (C) PAUL REVERE II, AAR, 1st ACD, 5 Sep 66, Doc. 10.
52. (C) Ibid.
53. (C) Interview with Capt Hoon, Doc. 4.
54. (C) Ibid.
55. (C) Ibid.
56. (C) Ibid.
57. (C) Ibid.
58. (C) Ibid.
59. (C) Ibid.
60. (C) Ibid.
61. (C) PAUL REVERE II, AAR, 1st ACD, 5 Sep 66, Doc. 10.
62. (C) Ibid.
63. (C) Ibid.
64. (C) PAUL REVERE II, AAR, 1st ACD, 25 Jan 67, Doc. 6.
65. (C) Ibid.
66. (C) Ibid.

CHAPTER III

1. (C) Combat Operations After Action Report, PAUL REVERE III, IV, 3d Bde, 25th Inf Div, 5 Nov 66, Doc. 12. (Hereafter cited: PAUL REVERE III AAR, 3/25, 5 Nov 66.)

2. (C) USAF/VNAF OPREP/JOPREP 5, 26-31 Aug 66.

3. (C) PAUL REVERE III, AAR, 3/25, 5 Nov 66, Doc. 12.

4. (C) Ibid.

5. (C) After Action Report, Operation 50, 14 Nov 66, Doc. 13.

6. (C) Ibid.

7. (C) Ibid.

8. (C) Ibid.

9. (C) Ibid.

10. (C) Ibid.

11. (C) Ibid.

12. (C) Ibid.

13. (C) Ibid.

14. (C) Ibid.

15. (C) Ibid.

16. (C) Ibid.

17. (C) Ibid.

18. (C) Ibid.

19. (C) Ibid.

20. (C) Ibid.

21. (C) Ibid.

22. (C) MACV MONEVAL, Dec 66.

CHAPTER IV

1. (C) After Action Report, PAUL REVERE IV, 4th Inf Div, 28 Jan 67, Doc. 14. (Hereafter cited: PAUL REVERE IV, AAR, 4th Div, 28 Jan 67.)

2. (C) Ibid.

3. (C) Ibid.

4. (C) Ibid.

5. (C) Ibid.

6. (C) PAUL REVERE III, AAR, 3/25, 5 Nov 66, Doc. 12.

7. (C) Interview with Capt Maxim, Doc. 8.

8. (C) PAUL REVERE IV, AAR, 4th Div, 28 Jan 67, Doc. 14.

9. (C) Ibid.

10. (C) PAUL REVERE III, AAR, 3/25, 5 Nov 66, Doc. 12.

11. (C) PAUL REVERE IV, AAR, 4th Div, 28 Jan 67, Doc. 14.

12. (C) Ibid.

13. (C) Ibid.

14. (C) Ibid.

15. (C) Ibid.

16. (C) PAUL REVERE III, AAR, 3/25, 5 Nov 66, Doc. 12.

17. (C) After Action Report, Operation PRONG, 8 Dec 66, Doc. 15. (Hereafter cited: Operation PRONG, AAR, 8 Dec 66.)

18. (C) Ibid.

19. (C) Ibid.

20. (C) Ibid.

21. (C) Ibid.

22. (C) Ibid.

23. (C) Ibid.
24. (C) Ibid.
25. (C) Ibid.
26. (C) Ibid.
27. (C) Ibid.
28. (C) Ibid.
29. (C) Ibid.
30. (C) Ibid.
31. (C) Ibid.
32. (C) Ibid.
33. (C) Ibid.
34. (C) Ibid.
35. (C) Ibid.
36. (C) Ibid.
37. (C) Ibid.
38. (C) Ibid.
39. (C) PAUL REVERE IV, AAR, 4th Div, 28 Jan 67, Doc. 14.
40. (C) Interview with Capt Charles D. Henderson, FAC, 2d Bde, 4th Inf Div, by Lawrence J. Hickey, Pleiku, 16 Feb 67, Doc. 16. (Hereafter cited: Interview with Capt Henderson.)
41. (C) Ibid.
42. (C) Ibid.
43. (C) Ibid.
44. (C) Ibid.
45. (C) Ibid.
46. (C) Ibid.

47. (C) Ibid.

48. (C) Ibid.

49. (C) Operation PRONG, AAR, 8 Dec 66, Doc. 15.

50. (C) Ibid.

51. (C) Ibid.

52. (C) PAUL REVERE IV, AAR, 4th Div, 28 Jan 67, Doc. 14.

53. (C) Ibid.

54. (C) Ibid; Interview with Capt Henderson, Doc. 16.

55. (C) PAUL REVERE IV, AAR, 4th Div, 28 Jan 67, Doc. 14.

56. (U) Interview with S/Sgt Frederick R. Schneider, Jr., Radio Operator, 2d Bde, 4th Div, by Lawrence J. Hickey, Plei Djereng, 17 Feb 67. (Hereafter cited: Interview with S/Sgt Schneider.)

57. (U) Ibid.

58. (U) Ibid.

59. (C) PAUL REVERE IV, AAR, 4th Div, 28 Jan 67, Doc. 14.

60. (C) Interview with 1st Lt James R. Thyng, Pilot, 1st ACS, by Lawrence J. Hickey, Pleiku, 18 Feb 67, Doc. 17. (Hereafter cited: Interview with 1st Lt Thyng.)

61. (C) Ibid.

62. (C) Ibid.

63. (C) Ibid.

64. (C) Ibid.

65. (C) Ibid.

66. (C) Ibid.

67. (C) Ibid.

68. (C) Ibid.

69. (U) Interview with S/Sgt Schneider.

70. (C) Interview with 1st Lt Thyng, Doc. 17.

71. (C) Interview with Capt Henderson, Doc. 16.

72. (C) Ibid.

73. (C) Ibid.

74. (C) Ibid.

75. (C) PAUL REVERE IV, AAR, 4th Div, 28 Jan 67, Doc. 14.

76. (C) Interview with 1st Lt Thyng, Doc. 17.

77. (U) Interview with Capt Paul E. Freeman, USA, S3, 1/12th, 4th Inf Div, by T/Sgt Chuck Ammusen, USAF, 14 Nov 66.

78. (U) PIO Interview with Lt Col James R. Lay, CO, 1/12th, 4th Inf Div, by T/Sgt Chuck Ammusen, USAF, 14 Nov 66.

79. (C) PAUL REVERE IV, AAR, 4th Div, 28 Jan 67, Doc. 14.

80. (C) Operation PRONG, AAR, 8 Dec 66, Doc. 15.

81. (C) PAUL REVERE IV, AAR, 4th Div, 28 Jan 67, Doc. 14.

82. (C) Ibid.

83. (C) Ibid.

84. (C) Ibid.

85. (C) Ibid.

86. (C) Ibid.

87. (C) Ibid.

88. (C) Ibid.

89. (C) Ibid.

90. (C) Interview with Capt Earl C Mizell, FAC, 2d Bde, 1st ACD, by Lawrence J. Hickey, New Phu Cat, 13 Jan 67, Doc. 18.

91. (C) Ibid.

92. (C) Ibid.

93. (C) Ibid.

94. (C) Ibid.

95. (C) Ibid.

96. (C) Ibid.

97. (C) Ibid.

98. (C) Ibid.

99. (C) Ibid.

100. (C) PAUL REVERE IV, AAR, 4th Div, 28 Jan 67, Doc. 14.

101. (C) Ibid.

102. (C) Ibid.

103. (C) Ibid.

104. (C) Ibid.

105. (C) MACV MONEVAL, Dec 66; Operation PRONG, AAF, 8 Dec 66, Doc. 15.

106. (C) PAUL REVERE IV, AAR, 4th Div, 28 Jan 67, Doc. 14; Operation PRONG, AAF, 8 Dec 66, Doc. 15.

CHAPTER V

1. (C) MACV MONEVAL Jan 67.

2. (C) MACV SITREP, 14 Feb 67.

3. (C) Interview with Capt Henderson, Doc. 16.

4. (C) Ibid.

5. (C) Ibid.

6. (C) MACV Daily Journal, 14 Feb 67; Interview with Capt Henderson, Doc. 16.

7. (C) Daily SITREP, 4th Inf Div, 15 Feb 67.

8. (C) Interview with Capt Henderson, Doc. 16.

9. (C) Interview with Maj Charles E. Rodgers, Pilot, 1st ACS, by Lawrence J. Hickey, Pleiku, 18 Feb 67, Doc. 19.

10. (C) Ibid.

11. (C) Ibid.

12. (C) Information provided Lawrence J. Hickey by LNO (Army) to 1st ACS, Pleiku, 18 Feb 67.

13. (C) Combat Operations After Action Report, SAM HOUSTON, 4th Inf Div, 16 May 67, Doc. 20. (Hereafter cited: SAM HOUSTON, AAR, 4th Div, 16 May 67.)

14. (C) Interview with Capt Noah E. Loy, FAC, 2d Bde, 4th Inf Div, by Lawrence J. Hickey, Pleiku, 18 Feb 67, Doc. 21.

15. (C) Ibid.

16. (C) Ibid.

17. (C) Ibid.

18. (C) SAM HOUSTON, AAR, 4th Div, 16 May 67, Doc. 20.

19. (C) Daily SITREP, 4th Div, 16 Feb 67; Notes compiled by Lawrence J. Hickey during Field Trip, Pleiku, 14-18 Feb 67.

20. (C) Notes compiled by Lawrence J. Hickey during Field Trip, Pleiku, 14-18 Feb 67.

21. (C) Ibid.

22. (C) SAM HOUSTON, AAR, 4th Div, 16 May 67, Doc. 20.

23. (C) Ibid.

24. (C) Ibid.

25. (C) Interview with Capt Eugene Fontinot, FAC, 2d Bde, 4th Inf Div, by Lawrence J. Hickey, Bien Hoa, 1 May 67, Doc. 22. (Hereafter cited: Interview with Capt Fontinot.)

26. (C) SAM HOUSTON, AAR, 4th Div, 16 May 67, Doc. 20.

27. (C) Ibid.

28. (C) Interview with Capt Fontinot, Doc. 22.

29. (C) SAM HOUSTON, AAR, 4th Div, 16 May 67, Doc. 20.

30. (C) Ibid.

31. (C) Ibid.

32. (C) Ibid.

33. (C) Ibid.

34. (C) Ibid.

35. (C) Ibid.

36. (C) Ibid.

37. (C) Ibid.

38. (C) Ibid.

39. (C) Ibid.

40. (C) Ibid.

41. (C) Ibid.

42. (C) Ibid.

43. (C) Ibid.

44. (C) Ibid.

45. (C) *Ibid.*
46. (C) *Ibid.*
47. (C) *Ibid.*
48. (C) *Ibid.*
49. (C) *Ibid.*
50. (C) *Ibid.*
51. (C) *Ibid.*
52. (C) *Ibid.*

APPENDIX I

USAF SUPPORT of PAUL REVERE II

1. Aircraft sorties

	Missions	Sorties
Immediate	79	145
Preplanned	214	452
Spooky (AC-47)	2	2
Arc Light (B-52)	5	N/A
Total	300	599

2. Ordnance*

	Quantity	Tons
GP	1,000	398
Napalm	218	53
Frag	720	38
Rockets	2,072	48
CBU	134	N/A
Total	4,144	537

* Excluding Arc Light

APPENDIX II

USAF SUPPORT OF PAUL REVERE IV

1. Aircraft Sorties

	Msns Req	Msns Flown	Sorties
FAC Immediate	303	286	645
Combat Proof Immed	141	93	176
FAC Preplanned	689	546	1,347
Combat Proof Preplanned	567	300	576
Spooky (AC-47)	61	51	51
Arc Light (B-52)	N/A	32	192
Total	1,761	1,308	2,987

2. Types of Aircraft

	A-1E	B-57	F-4C	F-100	NAVY USMC
FAC Immediate	193	26	97	277	52
Combat Proof Immed	-	26	118	32	-
FAC Preplanned	76	74	79	1,114	4
Combat Proof Preplanned	-	46	299	231	-
Total	269	172	593	1,654	56

3. Damage Assessment

	Huts	Bunkers	AA/AW	Sec Exp	Est KBA*
FAC Immed	120	58	20	17	21
Combat Proof Immed	-	-	-	1	-
FAC Preplanned	148	162	19	32	68
Combat Proof Preplanned	-	8	-	1	-
Total	268	228	39	51	89

* This figure does not include KBA from major ground engagements as all enemy bodies policed from the scene were listed as KIA.

APPENDIX III

USAF SUPPORT OF SAM HOUSTON

1. Aircraft Sorties

	Msns Req	Msns Flown	Sorties
FAC Immediate	196	217	473
Combat Proof Immed	38	29	57
FAC Preplanned	705	515	1,494
Combat Proof Preplanned	332	209	409
Spooky (AC-47)	76	67	67
Arc Light (B-52)	N/A	31	183
Total	1,347	1,068	2,683

2. Types of Aircraft

	A-1E	B-57	F-4C	F-100	NAVY USMC
FAC Immediate	106	14	84	269	-
Combat Proof Immed	-	-	5	52	-
FAC Preplanned	83	49	87	1,271	4
Combat Proof Preplanned	-	17	113	279	-
Total	189	80	289	1,871	4

3. Damage Assessment

	Huts	Bunkers	AA/AW	Sec Exp	Est KBA
FAC Immediate	36	71	11	24	92
Combat Proof Immed	-	-	-	1	-
FAC Preplanned	140	251	9	16	61
Combat Proof Preplanned	-	-	-	2	-
Total	176	322	20	43	153

4. Ordnance

	Quantity	Tons
Bombs (B-52)	N/A	3,567
Bombs (Fighters)	8,152	2,532
CBU	777	1,109
Napalm	3,396	1,033
Rockets	477	95
20-mm	262,842	66
7.62-mm (AC-47)	310,000	8
Total	585,644	8,410

GLOSSARY

AA	Antiaircraft
ACD	Air Cavalry Division
ADF	Automatic Direction Finder
ALO	Air Liaison Officer
AO	Area of Operation
ARA	Aerial Rocket Artillery
ARVN	Army of the Republic of Vietnam
AW	Automatic Weapons
BDA	Bomb Damage Assessment
Bn	Battalion
Cav	Cavalry
CBU	Cluster Bomb Unit
CIDG	Civilian Irregular Defense Group
Click	Kilometer
CP	Command Post
DAS	Direct Air Support
DASC	Direct Air Support Center
DF	Direction Finder
DFC	Distinguished Flying Cross
Div	Division
FAC	Forward Air Controller
Frag	Fragmented Operations Order
FSB	Fire Support Base
FWMAF	Free World Military Armed Forces
GM	Gravel Mine
GP	General Purpose
Inf	Infantry
KBA	Killed by Air
KIA	Killed in Action
KM	Kilometer
LOC	Line of Communication
LZ	Landing Zone

MG	Machine Gun
MIA	Missing in Action
mn	Millimeter
NVA	North Vietnamese Army
OPCON	Operational Control
PIO	Public Information Office
POW	Prisoner of War
Prep	Preparation
Recon	Reconnaissance
Regt	Regiment
ROK	Republic of Korea
SF	Special Forces
TAC	Tactical Air Command
TACP	Tactical Air Control Party
TAOR	Tactical Area of Responsibility
TFW	Tactical Fighter Wing
USAF	U.S. Air Force
USSF	U.S. Special Forces
VC	Viet Cong
VHF	Very High Frequency
VR	Visual Reconnaissance
VNAF	South Vietnamese Air Force
WIA	Wounded in Action
"Willy Pete"	White Phosphorous

www.ingramcontent.com/pod-product-compliance
Lightning Source LLC
Chambersburg PA
CBHW080549170426
43195CB00016B/2728